AQA GCSE
Computer Science

Student's Book

Steve Cushing

HODDER
EDUCATION

AQA GCSE Computer Science – Important information

Please note that when teaching the AQA GCSE Computer Science course, you must refer to AQA's specification as your definitive source of information. While this book has been written to match AQA's specification, it cannot provide complete coverage of every aspect of the course.

The Publishers would like to thank the following for permission to reproduce copyright material:

Photo credits: p4 *bl* Mark Evans/iStockphoto, *br* bloomua/Fotolia, *tl* masterpiece/Fotolia, *tc* Yordan Marinov/Fotolia, *tr* Siede Preis/Photodisc/Getty Images; **p11** Robert Gray; **p52** Photodisc/Getty Images; **p95** *c* Mark Evans/iStockphoto, *tl* Jakub Semeniuk/iStockphoto, *tr* Steve Connolly, *br* Siede Preis/Photodisc/Getty Images, *cr* Steve Connolly, *bl* Alysta/Fotolia; **p96** *tl* yuka26/Fotolia, *tr* Sweetym/iStockphoto, *bl* Mike McCune/iStockphoto, *br* Konstantin Shevtsov/Fotolia; **p99** malajscy/Fotolia.com; **p107** Godfried Edelman/iStockphoto; **p108** Robert Gray; **p112** Robert Gray; **p121** pizuttipics/Fotolia; **p122** bloomua/Fotolia; **p141** Robert Gray.

Every effort has been made to trace all copyright holders, but if any have been inadvertently overlooked the Publishers will be pleased to make the necessary arrangements at the first opportunity.

Hachette UK's policy is to use papers that are natural, renewable and recyclable products and made from wood grown in sustainable forests. The logging and manufacturing processes are expected to conform to the environmental regulations of the country of origin.

Orders: please contact Bookpoint Ltd, 130 Milton Park, Abingdon, Oxon OX14 4SB. Telephone: (44) 01235 827720. Fax: (44) 01235 400454. Lines are open 9.00–5.00, Monday to Saturday, with a 24-hour message answering service. Visit our website at www.hoddereducation.com

First published in 2013 by
Hodder Education, an Hachette UK company,
338 Euston Road
London NW1 3BH

Impression number   5 4 3 2

Year   2016 2015 2014 2013

Cover photo by ktsdesign/Fotolia
Illustrations by Gray Publishing
Typeset in ITC Berkeley Oldstyle 11/16pt and produced by Gray Publishing, Tunbridge Wells
Printed in Dubai

A catalogue record for this title is available from the British Library

ISBN 978 1444 18226 2

Contents

Chapter 1
Introduction

Before we begin

■ You should make sure that you have read and understood all of the content in each of the chapters of the book.

■ You should also read the relevant sections in AQA's specification for the course to ensure you have covered the relevant subject content.

■ You should attempt all of the tasks and questions within each section – they will help you to remember the information.

What is computer science?

Computer science is the study of modern computing devices and how they work. Computer science is also about problem solving. A good computer scientist needs to have a passion for finding solutions, an ability to use maths and to work creatively. If you like to solve games and puzzles, then computer science is for you!

A selection of modern computing devices. How many are you familiar with?

The use of computing technologies has never been so popular. Our lives are fully integrated into a computer science world of mobiles, tablet computers, desktop computers and laptop computers. It is hard to imagine our lives without a connection to the web. Originally, this connection was only available using a wired network. The invention of wireless systems such as WiFi (Wireless Fidelity), where the connection is through a router at home or through wireless hotspots, has changed the way we access and use the internet.

The biggest growth area in recent years has been in mobile data using what is termed cellular data networks. They are called cellular data networks because they use radio cells that are hexagonal-, circular- or square-shaped areas around radio masts. When you use your mobile you don't notice these cells but your mobile device switches from one to another as you move.

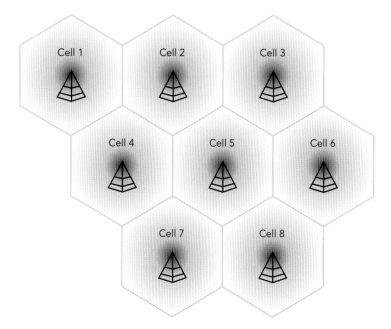

Mobile phone radio masts form a cellular network. Why do some people refer to their mobiles as cell phones?

What is a computer program?

A computer program is a sequence of instructions that enables a computer to do something. A computer can do nothing without being switched on and being given instructions. It does not matter what programming language is used as all the instructions are translated into codes that the computer can understand.

The first program a computer needs is an operating device called a bootstrap loader.

Most people will not attempt to write their own operating system program.

Key term

A wireless hotspot is simply a place where you can connect to WiFi. Many public places now have these hotspots.

Key term

A bootstrap loader is a program that exists in the computer's memory. It is automatically executed by the processor when the computer is switched on.

Once you have the operating system loaded and running, you will need software (or programs) for any tasks you want the computer to perform. If you only use your computer for word processing, playing games, internet browsing or other common tasks, there is a good chance you can buy or download the software you need. However, what happens when you need your computer to do something that all your shop-bought software cannot do?

All computing devices use programming to work. New developments in programming languages have led to an explosion in the use of device-independent social networks (social networks like Twitter and Facebook work on all different types of devices) and gaming. This has led to a fundamental change to our lives at work and home. Imagine a life without your mobile, games console or access to the internet.

Just a few years ago, computers were mysterious boxes hidden away in large, secure buildings. Most people only had experience of computers when their bank statements and electricity bills arrived through the post.

All that has now changed. Your understanding of computing will be as:

- A system that links sound, video, graphics and text to give you information and a means of communication, internet shopping, computer gaming and so much more.
- A hardly noticeable means of controlling everything from televisions to aeroplanes.

Task

Think about your day. List the places you visit and the things you do and write down all the things that involve a computer of some kind. Also remember to include all the computerised or computer-controlled things from central heating to the toaster.

Question

What is the purpose of an operating system?

The growth of the internet

The other big change has been the growth of the internet. When computers were first introduced they were boxes connected only to a power source. Now, most devices are becoming web enabled, which means that they are connected to each other by the internet. Even software applications are becoming 'cloud based'.

Key term

Cloud computing is the use of linked computing resources (hardware and software) over a network, usually the internet. Cloud computing is based on remote systems containing your data, software and social media systems.

This has fundamentally changed the way computer scientists think about computing and programming. New computer programming languages have appeared as a result of this new way of thinking.

With cloud computing you are not only surrounded by computers, but also surrounded by the data relating to you. Some of this data you create yourself on social networking sites, but some is also created when you open a bank account, enrol on a course, join a games site, have a mobile phone contract or shop on the internet.

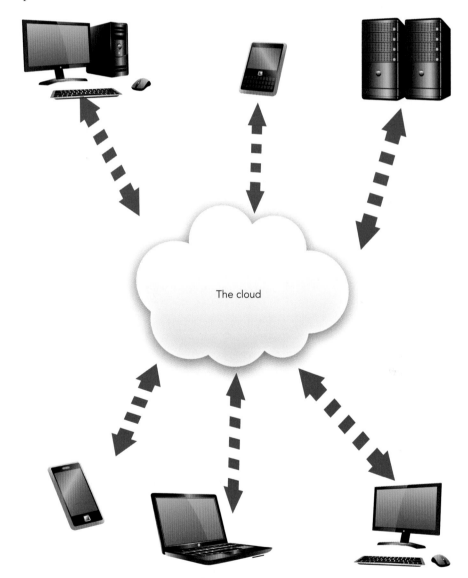

Computers can be connected to each other using the internet. What is the advantage of using programs stored in the cloud?

Task

What sort of information do nurses need during their working day?

Common computer languages in a connected world

This book will teach you about the basics of some of the most popular programming languages used today from Java and PHP to HTML5. The book starts by comparing different languages, for example, PHP and Python. This is to help you to see the similarities and differences. The language you or your teacher choose is not as important as understanding the concepts and principles of programming. In today's world, different languages are often used together, as you will discover as you work through the book.

What is open source software?

Open source refers to a program or software where the source code is available to the general public to use, and modify if they wish, free of charge.

Open source code is usually produced in collaboration, and groups of users and programmers improve on the code and share the changes with anyone else.

The opposite of open source is called proprietary software. This is privately owned: proprietary software is generally owned by a company.

PHP and HTML were originally designed for web development to produce dynamic web pages. PHP is a widely used open source software and is the alternative to proprietary software competitors such as Microsoft's ASP.

Diffferent types of open source PHP code and applications are available.

PHP

PHP is called a server scripting language. It is used to write web-based applications that make web pages interactive. When you edit a page on an interactive website, such as Wikipedia, and submit your changes, they are sent to one of the servers, where they are processed by PHP scripts. This language has been chosen for the book because it is at the heart of cloud computing.

> ### Task
>
> Look into the main uses of the following computer languages: PHP, Java, HTML5, Action Script, Python.

Java

Java is an object-oriented language and JavaScript is an object-based language. The names may sound the same but this often causes confusion to non-specialist programmers. In practice, there is a big difference between Java and

Key term

Source code is the actual code programmers use to write a program. It relates to all programming languages. When you write your own programs you will write the source code.

JavaScript. While both languages treat program elements as objects that can pass instructions to each other, Java is a true object-oriented language which uses inheritance. JavaScript cannot do this. The two languages also interact in very different ways with web pages and web browsers. You can use Java to create standalone applications and also to develop applets that run within a browser. JavaScript only works within a browser and as such you cannot use it to develop standalone applications. JavaScript code is placed within an HTML file and can perform various client-side functions.

Running/testing your own source code on your computer

Once you have written your code you will want to test it out on your computer. Some programming languages are easy to test. HTML and Java, for example, will just run in a web browser. But languages such as PHP are what are called 'server-side' programming languages, which means that they are designed to run on a web server and not on individual computers. You cannot just open the file in your web browser like you can with HTML and JavaScript.

Fortunately, there are lots of free programs you can use on your own computer to test PHP code without having to add it to a web server. It just means that you have to install extra software on your computer.

Key point

You should write your code in a text editor. Word processors like StarOffice and Microsoft Word are not designed to write computer programs. If you must use one of them for programming, make sure that you save your file as plain text. However, it is better always to use a text editor when writing code. You will also need to make sure that when you save the file, it has the correct extension. PHP, for example, needs to be .php not .txt, which is what most text editors save files as by default.

Machine language

Although you will be learning a programming language, computers only understand machine languages. While easily understood by computers, machine languages are almost impossible for humans to use because they consist entirely of numbers.

The language you learn will use almost the same instructions as a machine language but the instructions will have names instead of being just numbers.

Humans also use what are called denary (or decimal) numbers. Don't worry about the name, it just means that our numbers have a base of 10. Many people believe that we have a base 10 system because we originally learned to count using our fingers. Humans use the numerals 0, 1, 2, 3, 4, 5, 6, 7, 8 and 9.

Even though computers are based on a binary system, they have to convert the numbers into the denary system so that we can understand them.

'Hello World' in binary is:

```
0100100001100101011011000110110001101111001000000101011101101111
0111001001101100011001100100
```

or in another language the computer can understand, it is:

c7	3c	2a	3c	2a	2b	2a	5c	3c	28	5c	2a	2b	2a	5c	3c
28	5c	2a	2b	2a	5c	3c	28	5c	2a	2b	2a	5c	3c	28	5c
2a	2b	2a	5c	3c	28	5c	2a	2b	2a	5c	3c	28	5c	2a	2b
2a	5c	3c	28	5c	2a	2b	2a	5c	3c	28	5c	2a	2b	2a	5c
3c	28	5c	2a	2b	2a	5c	3c	28	5c	2a	2b	2a	5c	3c	28
5c	2a	2b	2a	5c	3c	28	5c	2a	2b	2a	5c	3c	28	5c	2a
2b	2a	00	00	01	00	00	00	00	00	00	00	00	00	00	00
00	00	00	00	00	00	00	00	00	00	00	00	00	00	00	00
00	00	00	00	00	00	00	00	00	00	00	00	00	00	00	00
00	00	00	00	00	00	00	00	00	00	00	00	00	00	00	00
00	00	00	00	00	00	00	00	00	00	00	00	00	00	00	00
00	00	00	00	00	00	00	00	00	00	00	00	00	00	00	00
00	00	00	00	00	00	00	64	48	65	6c	6c	6f	2c	20	57
6f	72	6c	64	21	00	00	00	00	00	00	00	00	00	00	00
00	00	00	00	00	00	00	00	00	00	00	00	00	00	00	00
00	00	00	00	00	00	00	00	00	00	00	00	00	00	00	00

Every central processing unit (CPU, the brains in the computer) has its own unique language (called machine language). Programs must be rewritten or compiled to work on different types of computers. Let's look at machine language in a little more detail.

Have you ever wondered why switches have a 1 for on and a 0 for off? It is based on binary computer code: 1 means 'on' and 0 means 'off'. Everything that a computer does is based on ones and zeros.

Imagine the computer is made up of switches, and each switch controls a light that can either be on or off: one or zero.

Question

What is a program written using binary codes called?

Each sequence of on-and-off lights could represent a different number. To explain the concept we will imagine that we have two lights, each with its own switch. They could be:

- both off
- first off, second on
- first on, second off
- both on.

Binary code takes each of these combinations and gives a number to it, like this:

- both off = 0
- first off, second on = 1
- first on, second off = 2
- both on = 3.

A switch. Why not just use 'on' and 'off' instead?

Maybe you are thinking that it would take rather a lot of switches and lights to make a computer work.

Imagine that we had six lights like this:

on   on   off   on   off   off

and rather than giving a light just one score, we give different lights in the sequence different scores: the first light 32, the second 16 then 8, 4, 2, 1. The point values of those six bulbs would be:

32 + 16 + 0 + 4 + 0 + 0 (remember: we only give points if they're turned on!)

and that adds up to 52. So we would say the sequence of lights is worth 52. But we would write it as: 110100 (that is on, on, off, on, off, off). This is how computers work and we call it binary code.

Computers can also use what are called hexadecimal numbers. There are 16 hexadecimal numbers. They look exactly the same as the decimal numbers up to 9, but then there are letters (A, B, C, D, E, F) in place of the denary numbers 10 to 15.

A single hexadecimal digit can show 16 different values instead of the normal 10 like this:

Decimal:	0	1	2	3	4	5	6	7	8	9	10	11	12	13	14	15
Hexadecimal:	0	1	2	3	4	5	6	7	8	9	A	B	C	D	E	F

Converting hexadecimal numbers is much harder than converting binary numbers. We have to work backwards to convert these numbers.

As an example, if we have a hexadecimal number of 1128 this is calculated as follows.

- The last number is 8. It represents $8 \times (16^0)$, which equals 8.

Key point

Any number to the power of 0 equals 1. We write powers in computing using the ^ symbol so 16 to the power 3 is written as 16^3.

- The next number is 2. This represents $2 \times (16^1) = 32$.
- The next number is 1. This will be $1 \times (16^2) = 256$.
- Finally, $1 \times (16^3) = 4096$.

If we add the totals together 1128 in hexadecimal = 4392 in denary.

You may also want to remember some of the powers of 16.

Power of 16	Result
16^0	1
16^1 = 16	16
16^2 = 16 ×1 6	256
16^3 = 16 × 16 × 16	4096
16^4 = 16 × 16 × 16 × 16	65536

You may be asking about the letters. They work the same way, so FA8 working backwards would be:

- $8 \times 1 = 8$
- $10 \times 16 = 160$ (remember A = 10 and this has to be multiplied by 16^1)
- $15 \times 256 = 3840$ (remember F = 15 and this has to be multiplied by 16^2).

The total in denary would be 4008.

You now know a little bit about machine language.

Questions

1   Write the binary code for the denary number 67. Use seven binary digits.
2   Give one reason why we use binary to represent data in computers.
3   State the denary representation of the hexadecimal number D48.

Hardware and software integration

Understanding machine language on its own is not enough; you need to look at the interaction between code (programming language) and databases/text files, prototyping, software development, computer models and websites. It is also necessary to understand the interactions between the code and the developments in computer hardware.

Programming

The first task a computer programmer learns is how to write a program that outputs 'Hello World'.

The simplest programming language to use is Python. In Python it would consist of a single line that tells the computer the command.

Start up your editor and save the following into a file and save your file as HelloWorld.py

```
print "Hello, World!"
```

You have just produced your first piece of code. Now let us look at how that is achieved in PHP.

```
<?php
print "Hello World";
?>
```

We are using PHP as an example throughout the book because PHP pages are HTML pages with PHP commands embedded in them. The web server processes the PHP commands and sends their output alongside any HTML to the browser. This makes PHP an ideal language for developing web applications.

We can achieve the same thing in PHP by:

```
<?php
echo "Hello World";
?>
```

Both print and echo are commands used to output information. Both do the same job, so it usually comes down to a matter of personal preference as to which one the programmer wants to use. Later, you will find that there is a difference, as by using the print command you could also return a true/false value. These more complex programming skills will be covered later.

Key point

When you write code in PHP or Java you need to declare what code you have used, otherwise the system will not understand it.

```
<?php
?>
```

These two simple declaration lines tell the PHP engine that everything between them is PHP code. Everything outside the two tags is treated as HTML and ignored by the PHP. The important point you need to remember is that PHP engine and Java scripts are embedded inside regular HTML pages.

As stated above, one of the advantages of PHP is that we can include HTML within the commands so we can write a whole web page by simply stating:

```
<html>
  <head>
    <title>Hello World</title>
  </head>

  <body>
    <?php print "Hello, World!" ?>
  </body>
</html>
```

Notice how the whole of the PHP code is in a single line embedded into the HTML code. You can spread a statement across any number of lines, or lump the statements together on a single line. For example, this statement:

```
<?php print "Hello, World!" ?>
```

Could be written:

```
<?php
print "Hello, World!"
?>
```

You are probably wondering how the code can be written in a single line, but in general, white space doesn't matter in a PHP program. However, it does matter if you are using Python, so be careful.

Programmers often add white space to make reading and correcting the code easier. You may even see the code written in a slightly different way:

```
<?php
    print ("Hello World");
?>
```

The output will be the same, it is just that some programmers like to put the output in brackets. You need to take time to understand the conventions of your own chosen language. You may also be wondering why the code print ("Hello World") is indented. Programmers use an indent with blocks of code to convey the program's structure. Indentation is not needed in most programming languages but it does help to show the structure of the code. The size of the indent is usually independent of the style. Some programmers use tabs for indentation.

Be careful with programming languages such as Python, because they use indentation to determine the structure instead of using other syntax or keywords.

Task
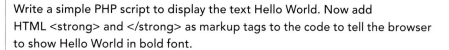

Write a simple PHP script to display the text Hello World. Now add HTML <strong> and </strong> as markup tags to the code to tell the browser to show Hello World in bold font.

As you learn programming you will develop your own style of writing code; just remember that you are trying to achieve the most efficient program. You will also need to go back to your code and edit it. Programmers often add comments to their code so that they know what each bit of code does. We will look at how we can do this in our Hello World program. There are a number of different ways we can add comments.

In Python you can use two methods:
- # for a single-line comment
- " " " for a multi-line comment which goes over many lines.

In PHP there are three methods of adding comments. The first is by using // to comment out a line. Here is an example:

```
<?php
  print "Hello World";
  //this is a comment
?>
<?php
```

We can only add a single-line comment using this method. Another option is to use a # sign as with Python. Here is an example of this:

```
<?php
  echo "Hello World";
  #this is a new comment
?>
```

When PHP encounters a hash mark (#) within the code, everything from the hash mark to the end of the line or the end of the section of PHP code (whichever comes first) is considered a comment. So you could add:

```
##############################
## My First Hello World Code
##############################
```

to make this part of your programming stand out.

If you have a longer, multi-line comment, the best way to comment is by using /* */. You can contain several lines of commenting inside a block. Many different languages use this method. Here is an example:

```
<?php
  echo "Hello World";
  /*
Using this method
you can create a larger block of text
and it will all be commented out
*/
?>
```

Key point

When you are using more than one line of code inside your PHP tags, remember to separate each line with a semicolon (;).

Task

Look into the different ways of adding comments in your chosen programming language.

You may think that comments are not needed, but almost all professional programmers have experience of having to edit their own work. This may be a year or two after they first wrote the code and they may first have to spend hours working out what they originally did. As you have already seen, there are many different ways a programmer can use code.

Comments can also remind you of what you were thinking at the time and, of course, are helpful to an examiner or other programmer who is checking your code.

Key point

Always add comments to your code so that you know what each piece of code is meant to do. How do you write good comments? In the beginning you can explain how everything works in comments as this may help you to remember what you have done.

Question

What is the difference between 'echo' and 'print' and what do they do?

Chapter 2
Constants, variables and data types

Introduction

As we study, we store what we learn in our brains. Some of the things that we learn, for example, how to walk, are stored permanently and we carry out the same actions each time. The data we need to do this is constant.

Other things we learn are always changing. While on holiday, for example, we may look at a set of directions to find the beach, but during the next holiday we will be in a different location and the instructions will be different; even on this holiday we will not always start from the same position. The data we need will be variable.

Most programming languages use what are called *variables* and *constants* to store these types of data.

Just like you, computer programs have to store data when carrying out actions and performing calculations. Imagine that you are lost on the way to the beach: you would need to look for buildings and landmarks that you recognise and work out which way to go. In the same way, a computer program may need to calculate a set of values, compare them, and perform different actions (called operations), depending on the result of the comparison.

> ### Task
>
> Write down five activities that you do each day that are constants: you always do them the same way.
>
> Now write down five things that are variables: you never do them the same way.

Data, information and knowledge

A common mistake is to interchange the terms *data*, *information* and *knowledge* when referring to the same thing. There are distinct differences between these three concepts.

Data could consist of facts or statistics used for analysis. It could be numbers, characters, symbols or images that are processed by a computer. In the same way, the buildings and landmarks you remember seeing on the way to the beach are no use without context. On its own, data carries no meaning. In order to take on some meaning, data must be interpreted or processed in some way by a human or machine.

When data takes on meaning, it becomes *information*. Information could be a sentence of words, a sequence of numbers or a series of images that have been put into a context, which is what gives the data meaning. Information can also be used to communicate, control and instruct. For example, you remember passing the tall building on your left last time you visited the beach and can see the tall tower in the distance that is next to the beach. Now the tower you can see in the distance has meaning.

Knowledge, however, is information about things, facts and concepts, that has been shared between people.

Let's look at an example. If Tommy finds out the height of the Eiffel Tower he has gathered some *data*; however, if he has a book describing what it is made out of and how it was built to that height, he has gained some *information*. Now, if he then tells his friends what he has learnt about the Eiffel Tower, it could be said that he is transferring *knowledge*.

Another example would be: VS051 0935 GRN is *data*. Virgin flight VS051 to Grenada departs at 9.35a.m. is the *information* you needed to go on your holiday.

If your friend shouted '75p' at you, you would be very confused, but if she shouted 'the drink costs 75p' you would understand.

Questions

1 See if you can identify which of the following are just data and which are information:
   ■ 65
   ■ NN126DD
   ■ 22 Harrow Lane.

2 Is a cooking recipe information or data according to the definitions given on the previous page?

What has this got to do with learning about computing?

Computers were invented because as humans we have always had an interest in data. We like to search for things and then to store, analyse, process and turn what we discover into information.

Computers are an ideal tool for doing this. They allow us to acquire data, store it, retrieve it and combine it with other data.

Input devices can remotely collect the data. Output devices allow us to present the results of this computer processing (that is, information).

Changing data into information

In order to change *data* into *information*, it needs to become part of a structure.

Steve decides to carry out a survey to find out how many of his friends know which city in France the Eiffel Tower is in. His first table looked like this:

Sam	Yes
Hussain	Yes
Jessica	No
Billy	Yes
Sinita	No
Timothy	No
Mike	Yes

The first column has a list of his friends' names and the second 'yes' or 'no' based on their answers to his question. You only know what the chart means because you know what he was doing. If you did not know what he was doing, the data in the table would be meaningless.

Steve now adds headings to the table.

Name of person questioned	Did they know in which city the Eiffel Tower stands?
Sam	Yes
Hussain	Yes
Jessica	No
Billy	Yes
Sinita	No
Timothy	No
Mike	Yes

By adding headings to his table, Steve has given the data within the table meaning. In other words, he has now changed the data into information. Anyone looking at the table will know that the first column of names is a list of the people he asked the question of, and the second column tells us: 'Yes, they did know in which city the Eiffel Tower is in' or 'No, they did not know in which city the Eiffel Tower is in'.

Data types

Before we look at what *constants* and *variables* are, we need to find out about *data types*. The most common of these, and the ones you will be using, are called primitive data types. Primitive data types are predefined types of data which are supported by the programming language.

So, we know that data can be stored in many different forms and that the proper term for these forms is *data types*. In computing, it is these forms that determine what actions, for instance searching, sorting or calculating, can be performed on the data when it is held within a field of a database or a spreadsheet.

Before we get back to coding, let's use this graphic to look at some of the common primitive data types that you will be using.

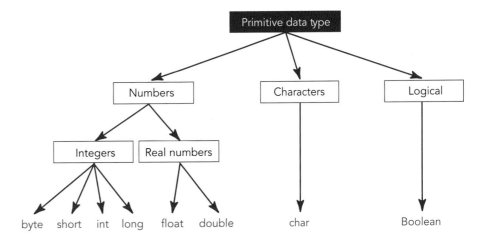

Common primitive data types.

Integer

Integer data types deal with whole numbers, not decimal numbers, which use a different data type. An integer is a whole number (not a fractional number) that can be positive, negative or zero.

Examples of integers could be: –9, 3, 5, 8, 98 and 5103. Examples of numbers that are not integers could be: –1.33, $1\frac{3}{4}$, 3.14 and 1500.45.

Question ❓

In mathematics, which of the following are integers?

6,   –7,   2.6,   10,   4.5,   17,   17.0

In PHP, integers can be specified in base 10, hexadecimal (base 16), octal (base 8) or binary (base 2) notation, and can be preceded by a sign (+ or –) to make them positive or negative.

```php
<?php
    $a = 1234; // decimal number
    $a = -123; // a negative number
    $a = 0123; // octal number (equivalent to 83 decimal)
    $a = 0x1A; // hexadecimal number (equivalent to 26
    decimal)
?>
```

Python can be forced to use a floating point:

```python
#this will force Python to return an integer rather than a float
int (17.0 / 8.0)
# this will force Python to return a float value.
float (17 / 8 )
```

Integers are usually sub-categorised in accordance with their capability for containing negative values. For example, within C and C++ the data type *unsigned short* can deal with whole numbers from 0 to 65,535, whereas *short* can deal with whole numbers from –32,768 to +32,767.

You will need to research your chosen programming language to see how it deals with integers.

Question ❓

What are the differences between 'integer' and 'real' data types?

Task

Look into how your chosen programming language deals with integers.

Real

A *real* data type contains numeric data in a decimal form. It is used in situations where more accurate information is required than an integer can provide (remember that an integer is a whole number).

A few examples of where a *real* data type may be used can be seen below:
- Distance in kilometres (km)   23.62, 3.51222, 109.33
- Speed in metres per second (m/s)   62.5, 10.2
- Weight in kilograms (kg)   20.666, 32.7

But *real* data types cannot store the actual measurement symbol (km, kg and so on) or the units of measurement, for instance kilometres or metres per second. If you want to use real data types you must remember to add the measurement symbol separately and print the units after the field displaying the data type.

It is worth noting that in the case of money (currency), the data type can be *real* or *integer*. For small values it is most likely that decimal places will need to be included and therefore a *real* data type is required. If the values being considered are large, such as the cost of houses, then it is doubtful that decimal places would be important, in which case only whole numbers would be considered and therefore the *integer* data type would be used.

You are perhaps asking yourself that if *real* data types can hold any number, what is the use of the *integer* data type? Well there are two reasons why the integer data type would be used.
- Processing speed: the time it takes a computer to calculate using 'real' numbers is a lot longer than using whole numbers held as integer data types.
- Storage: real data types take up more memory than integer data types; therefore if decimal points are not required it is more efficient to use integers.

One of the common problems encountered by people learning programming is choosing the wrong data types. The use of unsuitable data types can lead to programs behaving unexpectedly and lots of time being wasted in trying to understand what is going wrong.

Key point

Always check to ensure that you have chosen the correct data types.

Task

Look into how your chosen programming language deals with the real data type.

Boolean

The *Boolean* data type represents the values of true/false or yes/no. The primitive data type of a Boolean is logical. Boolean logic is a type of mathematical comparison. It is used to evaluate true or false. This may be new to you but it is not difficult to understand. Think back to Chapter 1 on binary numbers. The lights could be on = 1 or off = 0.

Consider the following sentence:

Key term

It is important to know that when we say print in a piece of code we don't actually mean print. The PHP engine never actually prints anything, it just displays it on your screen.

```
If white is a colour and snow is cold then print "ice
cream"
```

Notice how three expressions are being evaluated within this single sentence. First we have the two expressions:

```
If "white is a colour" AND "snow is cold"
```

The third is that Boolean logic evaluates each expression to see if it is either true or false.

```
if (true) And (true) then print "ice cream"
```

If you think back to the lights we could even write this as:

```
If colour = 1 cold = 1 then print
```

So now we know that Boolean logic is a type of arithmetic/comparison and that it is usually used in programming to return either a true or false action or a 1 for true and 0 for false.

```
If the sea is dark and the sky is grey then print "rain"
```

Most programming languages could understand this Boolean logic providing we add what are called parentheses:

```
If (the sea is dark) and (the sky is grey) then print
"rain"
```

Question

Identify the Boolean expressions in the following sentences:
- When the door is open and it is cold outside I have to wear my coat.
- The central heating switches off when it is warmer than 22°C and on when it is cooler than 18°C.

Task

Write down the way you get ready for school or college, using Boolean data types. Remember that you need simple but true statements for each thing you do.

Boolean logic evaluates every expression to either true or false. Therefore, substituting true or false for each of these expressions outputs the following:

```
if (true) And (true) then print "rain"
If (true And true) then print "rain"
```

If either statement was not true, nothing would be printed. Let's look at Boolean code in PHP:

```
<?php
  $true_value = true;
  $false_value = false;
  print ("true_value = " . $true_value);
  print (" false_value = " . $false_value);
?>
```

If you run this code you will find that the true value will print '1' and false value '0'. If you want to print 'true' rather than '1' you will need to add:

```
$true_value = true;
if ($true_value) {
print("that's true");
}
```

Boolean is very important as it is used often in programming, so make sure that you understand it.

In reality, the *Boolean* data type is hardly ever represented as a single binary digit even though only two values are possible. In fact, many programming languages don't necessarily have an explicit *Boolean* data type as it usually interprets 0 as false and any other value as true.

Task

Look at how your chosen programming language deals with Boolean.

Question

Write the following sentences as a Boolean expression:

'When the ground is too dry and the sun has gone down I water the plants. If the sun is hot and you water the plants it burns their leaves.'

Character primitive data types are held in what is called a string, so let's look at what a string is.

String

A string or text data type is capable of holding any alphanumeric character whether it is text, numbers or symbols. It is also capable of storing non-printable characters such as carriage returns as well as punctuation characters and spaces. The data contained within a string data type can either be pure text or consist of a combination of letters, numbers and symbols.

In Python we would define a string by:

```
astring = "Hello World!"
```

This defines the string astring as Hello World. Anything inside the quotes becomes the value of the string.

Many programming languages permit the storage of hundreds of characters as a single variable; however, in most situations the algorithm will be storing short string variables consisting of a couple of words.

It is important to note that when you use string data types to store numbers, you cannot perform any sort of mathematics on them. The sort of numbers that you would normally store as string data types would be things like telephone numbers where they often start with a zero – if you stored them as an integer, the zero would be deleted (remember that an integer cannot have a point, so 07 is stored as 7). As you never want to perform mathematical calculations on a telephone number, the string option is fine.

Question ?

Which of the following data would you store as an integer and which would you store as a string?

- Steve
- 15
- 007
- B901LK
- 2012
- 10.2
- Marks

Which is the odd one out and what would you store it as?

Date/time

The *date/time* data type is obviously used to store dates and times. The tricky aspect of this data type is that both dates and times can appear in many different forms. Also, some countries have different methods of representing the date, such as:

- 11/06/2014 means 6th November 2014 in the USA
- 11/06/2014 means 11th June 2014 in the UK.

The advantage of using the date/time data type is that you can choose which format you would like your date to be automatically displayed as, such as:

- 23/04/2014
- 23rd April 2014 or
- 23 April 2014 and so on.

Another advantage of using the *date/time* data type is that the data entered can be automatically validated. Validation makes sure that the data is valid, for example, in the correct format. It doesn't necessarily mean that it is accurate, just possibly accurate.

If you entered 30/02/2014 into a field assigned to accept a 'date' data type for example, it would automatically reject it and return an error message because there is no such date as the 30th February 2014 in UK format and no 30th month in the US format.

Constants and variables

Now, you know about *data types*, let's turn our attention back to *constants* and *variables*. You looked at what these were in your daily life, now it's time to look at them in terms of computer programming.

Key term

The contents, or values, of variables will change as users interact with the programs you write. This is why they are called variables.

Key term

A compiler is a special program that processes the lines of code you have written in your chosen programming language by turning them into the machine language or 'code' that the systems processor uses.

Variables

Throughout computer programming, variables are data entities whose values can be altered when a program is compiled. As their name implies, their values *vary*.

A *data entity* is a data model that has three parts: a structure, a collection of rules and the operators to be applied to the data.

A compiler is simply a computer program that translates a computer program written in one computer language (called the source language or source code) into an equivalent program written in another computer language (target language or output code).

The compiler produces a machine language program that can then be run on the computer. For example, Java uses a compiler to translate Java programs into Java Bytecode, which is a machine language for the Java Virtual Machine. Bytecode is similar to machine language, so it runs on the computer much more efficiently. Some computer languages don't use a compiler, but they are much slower as the language needs to be translated as it runs.

When you want the compiler to reserve an area of memory for some values used in your program, you must set a name, also often called an identifier. This will allow you to refer to that area of memory.

> **Key point**
>
> Most programs use various values which keep changing while the program is running. Values entered by one user will obviously be different from the values entered by another user. This means that when creating the program, you will not know all possible values that will be entered in your program by the user.

The name or identifier can be anything you choose but as with all programming there are clear rules you must follow. In programming the general rules are:

- The name of a variable can be as short as a single letter but not a single number.
- The name of a variable can start with a letter, or an underscore '_'.
- After the first character of the variable, the name of the variable can include letters, numbers or underscores in any combination.

- The name of a variable cannot be one of the words that the programming languages have reserved for their own use.

Let's consider some of the restricted words used in Java:

abstract	assert	boolean	break	byte
case	catch	char	class	const
continue	default	do	double	else
enum	extends	final	finally	float
for	goto	if	implements	import
instanceof	int	interface	long	native
new	package	private	protected	public
return	short	static	strictfp	super
switch	synchronized	this	throw	throws
transient	try	void	volatile	while

PHP has a different set of restricted words:

_halt_compiler( )	abstract	and	array( )	as
break	callable (as of PHP 5.4)	case	catch	class
clone	const	continue	declare	default
die( )	do	echo	else	elseif
empty( )	enddeclare	endfor	endforeach	endif
endswitch	endwhile	eval( )	exit( )	extends
final	for	foreach	function	global
goto (as of PHP 5.3)	if	implements	include	include_once
instanceof	insteadof (as of PHP 5.4)	interface	isset( )	list( )
namespace (as of PHP 5.3)	new	or	print	private
protected	public	require	require_once	return
static	switch	throw	trait (as of PHP 5.4)	try
unset( )	use	var	while	xor

All of these words perform a specific programming task within the Java and PHP languages so we cannot use them as a name for a variable. You will need to look at a list of restricted words for the language you choose to use.

Task

Research each of the specific words in your programming language's list of restricted words. What purpose do they each perform?

In Python, the operand to the left of the = operator is the name of the variable. The operand to the right of the = operator is the value stored in the variable. So, with this knowledge, let's look at how we can use a variable within program code. We must first 'define' it.

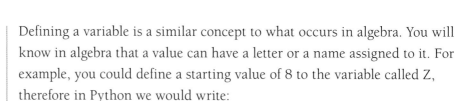

Defining a variable is a similar concept to what occurs in algebra. You will know in algebra that a value can have a letter or a name assigned to it. For example, you could define a starting value of 8 to the variable called Z, therefore in Python we would write:

```
Z = 8
```

Now at any point within a program where that value requires changing, it can be done by referring to the name of the variable Z. For example, if we state Z = 8, another part of the program then changes it by one of the following procedures, such as:

- Z = Z + 1, this adds 1 to the variable called Z, or
- Z = 5, which redefines the value called Z, or
- Z = Y + 1, which copies the value of another variable called Y, adds 1 and the answer becomes the redefined value of Z.

In computing terms we call this assigning, as we assign a value to Z.

So, do you understand the idea of variables now? The aim isn't to find out what the actual value of Z is, but to use Z as a storing place for values.

You can even define a group of variables or constants at the same time. Let's now put our knowledge to use with a PHP script to define a series of constants that you may use in your code in a single defined **array**:

```
<?php
...define(array(
  "second" => 1,
  "minute" => 60,
  "hour" => 3600,
  "day" => 86400,
  "week" => 604800,
  "month" => 2592000, // 30 days month
  "year" => 31536000,
  "year2" => 31622400
));
?>
```

Notice how PHP uses a different sign. As you become better at coding you will find that each language has its own method, but don't be put off by this: the basics of how it all works are the same and if you learn to code with an open mind you will be able to quickly modify your skills to suit different languages. This book has deliberately been written to help you to understand the concepts in a way that they will become transferable.

Key term

An array is a type of variable, but it's more like creating a box containing a group of variables within it. Unlike simple variables, arrays can contain more than one piece of data.

Task

Research how your chosen programming language defines a group of constants and create a simple program to define an array.

Key term

Constants store values, but as the name implies, those values remain constant throughout the execution of an application.

Constants are *data entities*, the values of which cannot change during a program's execution. As their name implies, their values are *constant*.

All data types can be declared as a constant. In programming, constants are very useful as they can make the source code simpler to understand. Also, if the value of the constant requires changing at some future point, then it only has to be done at the point where the constant is declared, which is usually at the beginning of the program.

Classes

A class is simply a description of an object. If you were making the object 'Car', the class would define the parts of a 'Car' (wheels, seats, steering wheel, engine) and things you can do with the object (drive, race, crash, park, clean).

Key point

The names of user-defined classes and functions, as well as built-in keywords such as echo, while, class, and so on, are not case sensitive in PHP, so these three lines are the same:

```
echo("Hello, World");
ECHO("Hello, World");
EcHo("Hello, World");
```

Let's look at an example involving a constant that you will be familiar with from maths: the constant π (pi).

Declare the code and define the constant π within your program:

```php
<?php
  define('PI', '3.14');
?>
```

If we now define radius:

```php
<?php
  define('radius', '6');
?>
```

You can now insert the constant's name, 'PI', into the program code at any instance where you require that value, such as when you need to work out the area of a circle:

```php
<?php
  $circleArea = PI * (radius * radius);
  print $circleArea;
?>
```

You will notice that the answer to π × (radius × radius) is $circleArea; $ is used to show a variable in PHP.

Now, say you wished to make the calculations within your program more accurate, to more decimal places. All you need to do is change the number at the instance within the source code where you defined the constant, for example:

```php
<?php
  define('PI', '3.1415926');
?>
```

There is no need to change any other lines of program code.

The 'define' instruction tells the computer what the constant is. In PHP, we use the $ sign where there is a variable. You can interchange these providing you remember what you used in the code, but the $ sign variable is a little slower to run than the define method. In practice, it all happens in milliseconds so that you will not notice the difference.

Constants and variables can also be used with character or string data types, such as:

```php
<?php
  $MYNAME = "Steve Cushing";
?>
```

Now, at every instance that 'Steve Cushing' needs to appear on the screen, or even on a printout, the variable '$MYNAME' is used. It can also be written as:

```php
<?php
  define('MYNAME', 'Steve Cushing');
?>
```

Again, at every instance that 'Steve Cushing' needs to appear on the screen, or on a printout, the constant 'MYNAME' is used.

A common error that programmers sometimes make is in not using the same capitalisation in a variable. Variables are case sensitive:

- $myname
- $MYNAME
- $Myname.

These three examples are all *different* variables. If you capitalise your variable in different ways throughout your code the program will not work.

Key point

Naming your functions and variables clearly is essential. You won't then need to explain how something works or what a particular function does. The name will tell the person reading the code what it does. Anything that can help another programmer or you to better understand your code is worth doing.

Unfortunately, there is no standard method of defining a constant. Each programming language has a different way of carrying out the procedure.

Should you attempt to change the value of a constant somewhere within the program code, the debugging tool will usually identify the error and inform you. So it is best to use a variable where there are likely to be changes.

Task

Research the methods of naming a constant in the programming language you will be using.

Constant naming convention

Constants, just as with variables, can be given almost any name and we can define them in PHP using define or $. However, as we can use the variable command $ for a constant, a very popular convention is to use all capital letters for naming constants and lower case for variables as shown below:

```php
<?php
  $MYNAME = "Steve Cushing";
  $steves_message = "Good morning from";
  print $steves_message." ". $MYNAME;
?>
```

This code displays 'Good morning from Steve Cushing' on a screen. Notice how the constant $MYNAME is in capitals and the variable $steves_message is in lower case, but that both have been defined using the $ variable.

The reason for using this convention is that it allows constants to be clearly distinguishable from variables within the program code.

You may be wondering what the semicolons are for. They separate simple statements. Unlike other languages, in PHP the semicolon before the closing statement and before ?> is not optional: you must put it there. This is why you need to study your chosen code very carefully, as small syntax errors will stop your program from running. You should look at the conventions used in your chosen code and learn them. Many programmers have spent hours not understanding why their code does not work, only to discover that a simple punctuation error was the reason.

A compound statement often uses curly braces to mark a block of code, such as a conditional test or loop that we will look at later. In these instances in PHP you do not need a semicolon after closing.

Key point

Programmers draft out their code on paper before typing it into a computer. You should draft out the code and check it away from the computer first.

Boolean expressions

As we considered earlier, Boolean expressions are expressions that result in a Boolean value, meaning a value that is either *true* or *false*.

In PHP, Boolean expressions are made up of the following Boolean operators:

Name of operator	Code operator in PHP	What it means
AND	&&	True if and only if both sides are true
OR	||	True if either side is true (or both are true)
NOT	!	Changes true to false and false to true

Here are some simple examples in code to make things a little clearer:

Wet AND Cold	`$wet && $cold`
Rich OR Poor	`$rich || $poor`
NOT happy	`!$happy`

You should now recognise the variables $wet, $cold and so on (variables because of the $ sign and the use of lower-case letters) and the use of && (as Boolean AND).

We can use brackets (or parentheses) to group complex Boolean expressions together. We looked at the use of brackets in Chapter 1. They are used to help the programmer and anyone else reading the code, but here they have a different use as the OR Boolean code has been used.

Take a look at these code examples:

```
If (($wet && $cold) || ($poor && $hungry)) {
  Print "I'm sad!";
}
```

The 'print' statement will be executed if the wet AND cold are both true OR if the poor AND hungry are both true.

There are, in fact, six arithmetic tests that can be used to create Boolean values. These are as follows:

Operator	Name of operator
<	Less than
<=	Less than or equal to
==	Equal to
!=	Not equal to
>=	Greater than or equal to
>	Greater than

All the operators within the above table have obvious meanings and can be used together with Boolean operators within conditional statements, such as:

```
if ($answer < 0 || $answer > 50) {
  print "The answer has an invalid value.";
}
```

Another example of a conditional statement using Boolean operators could be where you may want to test whether a variable 'i' lies between 1 and 10, such as:

```
if ($i >0 && $i < 11) {
}
```

Task

Write a simple piece of code in your chosen programming language that uses at least two Boolean operators.

Style within Boolean expressions

There is also a 'style' in using Boolean expressions that you should be aware of and use. Let's have a look a couple of statements, using code, that are written in both a poor and a good style.

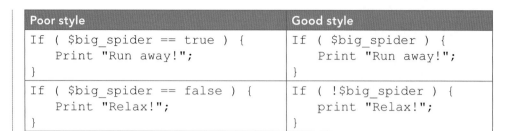

Poor style	Good style

`If ( $big_spider == true ) {`
`    Print "Run away!";`
`}`
	`If ( $big_spider ) {`
	`    Print "Run away!";`
	`}`

`If ( $big_spider == false ) {`
`    Print "Relax!";`
`}`
	`If ( !$big_spider ) {`
	`    print "Relax!";`
	`}`

What the table above demonstrates is that it is poor style to compare a condition to true or false as it appears a little silly.

Another aspect of style that should be avoided is the use of double negations, as the table below demonstrates:

Poor style	Good style

`If ( !$big_spider ) {`
`    print "Relax!";`
`}`
`else {`
`    print "Run away!";`
`}`
	`If ( $big_spider ) {`
	`    Print "Run away!";`
	`}`
	`else {`
	`    print ("relax!");`
	`}`

`If ( !$illegalmove($i,$j )) {`
`    move ($i,$j);`
`}`
	`If ($legalmove($i, $j)) {`
	`    move ($i, $j);`
	`}`

As you can see from the examples above, to avoid double negations, Boolean expressions should always be given positive names such as legalMove and gameOver rather than negative versions such as illegalMove and gameNotOver.

Task 1

Write out on paper a short piece of code where the answer is tested to see if it is between 4 and 8 using a Boolean conditioning statement within your code.

Task 2

Write a program to calculate the area of a simple shape such as a rectangle. The length of the sides could be constants and the area a variable.

Extension task

Write a simple program where the user can input the length of the sides of the simple shape.

Chapter 3
Structures

Specification coverage

- How data types can be combined to make data structures
- How data structures can make coding a solution to a problem simpler

Learning outcomes

- You should be able to explain what a data structure is.
- You should be able to produce your own data types that go beyond the built-in structures of the languages you are using, such as arrays or lists.
- Understand and be able to explain why data structures can make coding a solution simpler.

Introduction

Computer programming is all about creating a set of instructions to complete a specific task. You do this in your everyday life, you just don't think of it in a programming way. Let us look at an example. You get home from school and want to make yourself a jam sandwich. You know that you will first need to get two slices of bread, butter each piece, spread the jam, and finally put the two together. You cannot put the jam on the bread first or put the slices of bread together before you spread the butter and jam, everything has to be done in the correct sequence.

In this sense, your life is full of sequences, and you are always programming sequences in your head. To create any meal you have to follow a recipe. A recipe, like a correctly sequenced program, is useful for replicating an action.

Programs are not only useful for reproducing set actions that always follow the same order. Even young children re-create quite complex programming. When they play games such as rock, paper, scissors they are creating what is called an 'if' statement. If you have rock and I have paper, I win. But if you have rock and I have scissors you win. This simple game has all of the elements of a program. It is a set of sequences and actions performed based on the outcome of what is called a process and then repetition (once the game is complete you start again). We will look at this game in more detail later in the book.

In the context of computing, programming means creating a set of instructions not for a human to follow but for a computer to perform. These actions are performed to accomplish a specific task.

In this chapter we will look at programming sequences using a programming language that both you, as programmer, and the computer's operating system can understand.

Basic programming concepts

In computer programming you have to first work out the correct sequence of the commands. This may sound easy but let's look at a simple example to show how careful you need to be.

If you write down your friend's postal address it may look like this:

John Smith
22 Holly Road
Hempton
London

You know that this is the order that you should write an address, but this is the exact opposite of the way that the postal system works. Royal Mail needs to know the address in the logical task order. This means the order that you process the address: city first, next the area, then the road, and then the house number.

In some countries, the conventional order follows the logical task order. In Russia, letters are addressed in exactly the opposite order to the UK with the city first.

Postcodes were introduced to make better use of computerised systems. Postcodes work in the correct order. The first two letters refer to a town, except in London where they are compass points. Your friend's postcode could be: SW21 7HH.

The second half of your friend's postcode identifies the street. Usually, there will be two postcodes per street: one for the even numbers like your friend's address, and one for houses with odd numbers. Longer streets often have multiple postcodes.

For your programs to work correctly, all the commands have to be there *and* they need to be in the correct order, just like with the postcode.

Key point

Many computer programmers label their files using the date format of year, month, day as this is the logical way to automatically list them. The year is the first piece of data required, the month the next and finally the day. This is because there can be 12 files with the same day number in a single year.

Question

Create a set of statements for the following sentence and put them in a logical processing sequence.

'I get up early and open all my presents on Christmas Day. My dad creeps into my room hoping not to wake me late at night, but I often just pretend to be asleep. It's their fault really as they insist that I go to bed early on Christmas Eve.'

We can use sentences to show structures or we can use diagrams. We will look at how to use diagrams in the next chapter. First, we will look at data structures in computer programming in more detail.

Data structures

The study of data structures is about organising data so that it is suitable for computer processing. As we have seen in the introduction, this is one of the most important aspects of computer science.

Computer hardware looks at storage devices like internal memory and disks as holders of elementary data units (bytes), each accessible through its address (usually an integer).

Most data structures can be viewed as simple containers that can be used to store a collection of objects of a given type. The container could be a sentence. The objects (actions within the sentence) are called the elements of the container.

You will have thought about data structures when you first learned about computers. The files and folders that you use are part of a simple data structure, in the same way programmers have to think about the data structure in the code. With your friend's postal address, the city has areas, the areas have roads, roads have houses and your friend is one of the people in a particular house.

Defining data structures

A data structure can be defined as a collection of different data elements, which are stored together in a clear, structured form.

In programming, one of the most important design decisions involves choosing which data structure to use. *Arrays* and *linked lists* are among the most common data structures, and each is applicable in different situations.

Arrays and linked lists are both designed to store multiple elements, most often of the same type. An array is an ordered arrangement of data elements that are accessed by referencing their location within the array. A linked list is a group of elements, each of which contains a pointer that **concurrently** points to the following element.

Why do we use data structures?

It is fair to say that data structures are used in almost all of today's programs or software solutions as they provide a method of managing huge amounts of data efficiently. For example, this could be in a large database or an internet-indexing service. In most programming situations, efficient data structures are a key to designing efficient algorithms. In fact, some formal software design methods and programming languages emphasise data structures, rather than algorithms, because they are regarded as the key organising factors in software design.

Data structures: arrays

There are situations during the writing of code when programmers need to hold related data as a single item, for example, a list of employee names or makes of car. One method of doing this would be to assign a variable to each item in the list, such as:

```
$name = "Jim" in PHP or
name = "Jim" in Python
```

```
$girl = "Susan" in PHP or
girl = "Susan" in Python
```

```
$man = "Bill" in PHP or
man = "Bill" in Python
```

and so on.

Now, although this method does work, what if you wanted to find out what the second name was? The answer is that with this system you have no way of knowing, as there is no positional information contained within the assigned variables. To be able to this we need what is called a one-dimensional array.

Key term

Concurrently means happening at the same time as something else.

Key point

A one-dimensional array is a list of variables. To create an array, you first must define an array variable of the desired type.

One-dimensional arrays

One-dimensional arrays in Python and PHP are a data structure that allows a list of items to be stored with the capability of accessing each item by pointing to its location within the array. For example:

```
carMakers = ["Ford", "Land Rover", "Vauxhall", "Nissan",
"Toyota"]
```

or

```
<?php
  $carMakers = array[Ford, Land Rover, Vauxhall, Nissan,
  Toyota];
?>
```

The first line of code defines a variable, called 'carMakers', as an array, which is storing a number of items. Now, let's say that you wish to access the fourth car make (Nissan). What you do is use a position number, for example:

```
<?php
  $car_name = carMakers[3];
?>
```

This line of code will return the fourth car make in the array. The process of using a position number is called *indexing* and the position number is called the *index*. The items within the array are called the array *elements*.

The reason why this type of array is referred to as a one-dimensional array is because it only uses a single number to point to the position of array elements.

Question

Explain the term one-dimensional array.

Key point

It is worth noting that it is common practice within programming for the first element within an array to be given an index of zero rather than one, because zero is considered by most mathematicians to be a real number between –1 and 1. So in languages where arrays are positively indexed, zero is the first number (–1 is not possible, the first possible value then is 0).

In the 'carMakers' example on the previous page the elements would be indexed as follows:

`$car_name = carMakers[0];`	(would return Ford)
`$car_name = carMakers[1];`	(would return Land Rover)
`$car_name = carMakers[2];`	(would return Vauxhall)
`$car_name = carMakers[3];`	(would return Nissan)
`$car_name = carMakers[4];`	(would return Toyota)

Table arrays

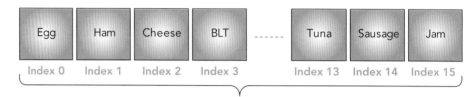

A tableData array showing for **16** different types of sandwich.

Sometimes arrays are stored separately. In a table array, just as we explored above, each of the array elements is identified or accessed by an index. An array with 10 elements will have indices from 0 to 9. That means, tableData[0] returns the first element of the tableData array. An element is identified using a pointer. The code *points* to the element.

Two-dimensional arrays

Two-dimensional arrays are a little more complex than the one-dimensional versions, but really they are nothing more than an array of arrays. In other words, there is an array in one row and another in the next row.

The best way of understanding a two-dimensional array is to think of it as a way of holding and accessing information within a matrix or grid made up of rows and columns, such as the one below:

	0	1	2	3
0	A	B	C	D
1	E	F	G	H
2	I	J	K	L
3	M	N	O	P
4	Q	R	S	T

Let's give this array the name 'letters'. Notice that we have five rows and four columns.

If you wished to define this two-dimensional array as a data structure, in code you would write it as follows:

```
$letters[5][4];
```

Key point

In PHP, as with variables, arrays are CaSe SenSItiVe. In PHP, variables must start with a letter or an underscore and not a number and are always defined with a $.

What we have here is the name of the array – 'letters' followed by a declaration (in square brackets) of how many arrays there are within the main array, which in this case is five (0–4) and finally a declaration (again in square brackets) of how many elements there are in each of the sub-arrays, which in this case is four (A, B, C, D or E, F, G, H, for example).

The output from the array looks like this:

Letters [0] [0]	and returns element 'A'
Letters [0] [1]	and returns element 'B'
Letters [0] [2]	and returns element 'C'
Letters [0] [3]	and returns element 'D'
Letters [1] [0]	and returns element 'E'
Letters [1] [1]	and returns element 'F'

We can even use this type of array to define an image. Think about the pixels in a digital photograph.

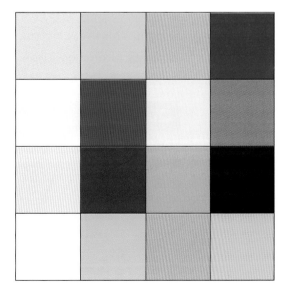

This is how a colour photograph's pixels look when viewed close up.

A digital photograph is simply a two-dimensional array. Conceptually, the pixel values for any image would be represented as a two-dimensional array. The number of columns corresponds to the width of the image (in pixels) and the number of rows corresponds to the height of the image (also in pixels). For example, an image that is 640 pixels wide by 480 pixels high would be stored in memory as a two-dimensional array having 640 columns and 480 rows. These two-dimensional arrays are often used in gaming as well.

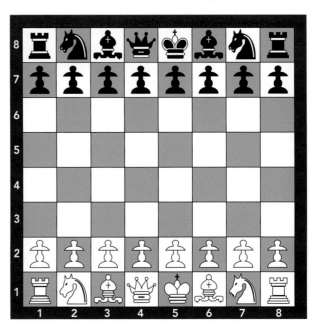

A chess board.

Let's assume that we want to store information about the chess board above.

We want to store information about what pieces are in which locations. The most natural way to store it would be to index locations by the row and column. This is easily done with a two-dimensional array and to access the elements within your two-dimensional array you would need to write a small looping routine.

Question

Explain the difference between single- and two-dimensional arrays.

Task

Identify the pieces in the game below using a two-dimensional array.

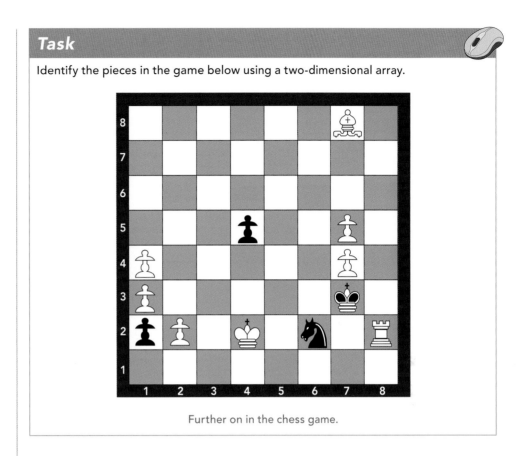

Further on in the chess game.

Representing lists

Data structures: linked lists

Linked lists are by their very nature one-dimensional. They can appear as *singly* linked lists or doubly linked lists as shown below.

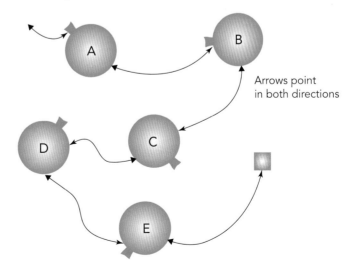

Arrows point in both directions

A representation of a doubly linked list.

A *singly* linked list is where the list can be done in one direction and to show this arrows (called element pointers) have one arrow with the element pointer pointing to the next element only. The diagram on the previous page shows a *doubly* linked list, where each element's pointer points both to the next element in the sequence and to the previous element.

Imagine that you have a set of drawers for your clothes. The first drawer has socks, the second T-shirts and so on. In a linked list, the drawers can only be opened in sequence: the first drawer then the second drawer and so on. With a doubly linked list you can go backwards and forwards but not miss out a drawer in the sequence.

The problem with linked lists is the way that they allocate computer memory. A linked list allocates a space for each element separately in its own block of memory called a *linked list element* or *node*. Just like your chest of drawers, they have a fixed size: you use the same amount of space in your sock drawer even if you only have one pair of socks. The list gets its overall structure by using pointers to connect all its nodes together like the links in a chain.

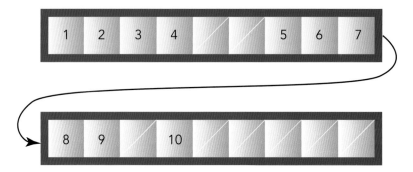

A representation of a singly linked list.

Data structures: binary search trees

Linked lists, like with our chest of drawers example, require a searcher to examine the entire chest of drawers, one drawer at a time.

An *index* is usually associated with a large, randomly accessed file in a computer system. This, like labels on your drawers, speeds retrieval by directing you to the small part of the file containing the desired item. If you wanted to wear only red clothes, you would need to examine each drawer in sequence in a linked list structure.

In computer science a binary tree is a data structure of *nodes* or junctions that is constructed in a hierarchy. Each node is joined to two *child nodes* at the most and every binary tree has a *root* from which the first two child nodes are connected. The child nodes are called the left child node and the right child node.

Now, if a node has no children, then these nodes are usually called *leaves*, and mark the end of the tree structure at that point.

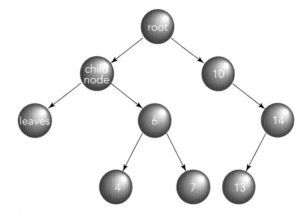

A simple binary tree.

There is a particular kind of binary tree, called the binary search tree or BST. BSTs are very useful for storing data for the purpose of rapid access, storage and deletion.

Task

Design a simple binary search tree to show the party game of putting the tail on the donkey. Each guest is blindfolded in turn and led to the donkey, they spin round four times, then they have to pin the tail on the donkey. The one who has put their tail closest to the X is the winner.

Question

Draw a binary tree to show the possible outcomes of tossing a coin eight separate times in terms of heads and tails.

Data in a BST are stored in tree nodes and must have a value or key associated with them. These keys are important because they are used to structure the tree so that the value of a left child node is less than that of the parent node and the value of a right child node is greater than that of the parent node. Typical key values include simple integers or strings. The actual data for the key will depend on the program being written and the language used.

BTrees

A further development from the binary tree is the BTree. There is no single scheme that is the best representation for all applications, but the BTree structure has become the most widely used.

The BTree is now the standard organisation for indexes in a database system. The BTree is the same as the binary tree but it can have more than two child nodes.

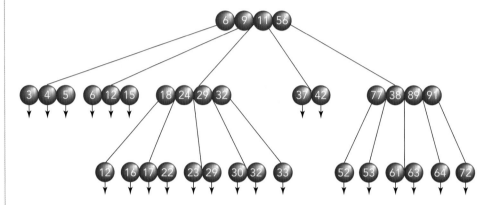

A example of a BTree.

Let us think about why all of this is important to computer scientists.

The key (K) in your clothes drawers might be a five-digit number, while the associated information, called a record (R), might consist of the type of colour, clothing, size, popularity and year purchased.

The key is only a five-digit number, so it is much shorter than listing all the information contained in the record. But we have so many different types of clothes that each needs a separate key. All the keys together would be too large to fit into the computer's temporary memory. We will learn about different memory types in later chapters, but for now you just need to know that the temporary memory has to fetch information from another slower memory source.

To help speed up the retrieval of this information we would need to construct an index.

Finally, let's assume that the keys, K, have a natural alphabetical order, so that we can refer to the *key-sequence order of* a file.

As we buy new clothes, we will have to insert, delete, retrieve and update our records. A set of *basic operations* that support such transactions are:
- add a new record, checking that K is unique
- remove a record K
- retrieve and find data.

Memory allocation

Memory management on nearly all types of computer is handled in a request and release fashion. An application says to the operating system, 'I would like some bytes of memory to use as I please.' If there is space available, the operating system gives a block of memory to the program and makes a note not to give that same memory out to anyone else. This process is called a *declaration* in computer programming. It is when you define the properties of variables or functions used in the program.

Most programming languages require you to *declare* the variables you intend to use in your program before they are used in any calculations or other operations.

When the application has finished with the memory it requested, the program is expected to return it to the operating system so that it can be allocated to another program.

If the program doesn't give the memory back, the operating system does not know if it's still needed so it cannot allocate it to another process. If a block of memory is not freed up, and the owning application has lost track of it, then it's said to have 'leaked' and is no longer available to anyone.

In most situations, program arrays are regarded as static, which means that their size is fixed and was defined when the program made a declaration. The blocks of memory allocated to each array tend to be situated next to each other on the storage media. Arrays, therefore, are typically used when the maximum number of elements is known at the design stage.

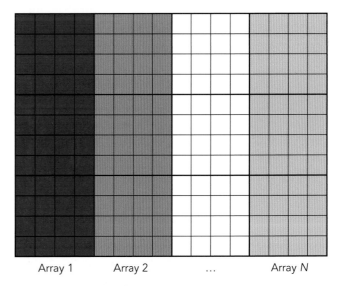

A diagram representing memory blocks.

The disadvantage to this approach is that large arrays require large amounts of memory, which can result in big chunks of memory not being used. This is especially the case when you have arrays in your program that are designed for a maximum number of data elements that will often never get anywhere near their capacity. It is like the sock drawer that was mentioned earlier always being empty when your T-shirt drawer is too small, but you cannot put your T-shirts in the sock drawer.

There are also some computer platforms, such as mobile devices, that, due to memory constraints, may even have limits on the size of array that you can use.

We now turn our attention to linked lists. These are regarded as dynamic. That means that when the program is run, they can shrink and grow as required.

Task

Find out about the different types of memory used in computing.

Question

Explain, using examples, the problems associated with memory allocation in computing.

As a consequence of being dynamic, linked lists tend to be more appealing when the number of data elements is unknown. In a linked list, allocated memory is scattered, and the program does not need to worry about needing a continuous memory block. Elements of memory can also be easily removed by breaking and rejoining the links. Also, as linked list memory is allocated on an element-by-element basis, the allocations are rarely next to one another within the storage media.

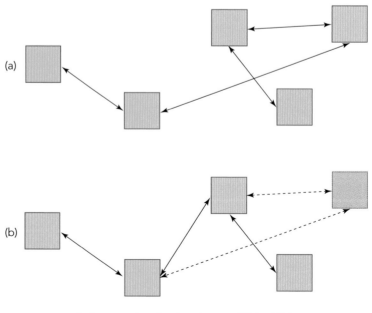

A diagram showing two types of linked list.

The disadvantage with linked lists having this capability to deal with uncertainty is that due to all the adding and deleting, there is a requirement for more programming time. Merely assigning to pre-allocated array elements is much quicker.

> **Key point**
>
> Memory allocation is the act of reserving a piece of memory for data. In programming terms, this is normally achieved by declaring a variable. Large arrays of data will require large blocks of contiguous memory, which the programmer needs to request from the operating system.

Accessing elements

As we have seen, elements within arrays are accessed by the process of *indexing* and therefore accessing the data is easy and fast – if you know which element you want to retrieve.

There are, however, situations where the elements are sorted based on some key value and specific elements are located using highly efficient search algorithms. These algorithms allow only a minimal number of comparisons to locate a unique element. Arrays, however, are inefficient when the ordering of their elements is likely to change because maintaining a sorted array when an element has been deleted or inserted could require the transfer of every element in the array!

In the case of linked lists, the contents are usually checked element by element until a match is found. This is because as a consequence of the memory for linked lists not necessarily being situated in a sequence, this list traversal process is the only method for searching the list (without using other data structures as part of the indexing process). The advantage of using disbursed memory is that reordering the list simply involves manipulating the links. The insertion or deletion of an element requires only a couple of pointer modifications. The transfer of the actual data isn't required at all.

Chapter 4
Program flow control

Specification coverage

- Sequencing
- Selection
- Iteration

Learning outcomes

- Understand the need for structure when designing coded solutions to problems.
- Understand how problems can be broken down into smaller problems and how these steps can be represented by the use of devices such as flowcharts and structure diagrams.
- Understand and be able to describe the basic building blocks of coded solutions (sequencing, selection and iteration).
- Know when to use the different flow control blocks (sequencing, selection and iteration) to solve a problem.

Introduction

In Chapter 3 we saw the importance of sequences. In this chapter we will explore ways of representing these sequences. If you think back we started with a simple sequence, making a jam sandwich. We then went on to look at the game rock, paper, scissors.

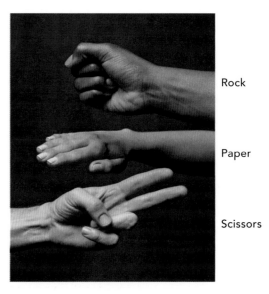

Rock

Paper

Scissors

Rock, paper, scissors game. A looping structure.

If the first player is a rock and the second scissors, the first player wins, but IF the second player is paper THEN they win.

This game led to one outcome or sequence of events to be executed if a statement was true, and another outcome or sequence of events to be triggered if the statement was false.

Task

Produce a looping sequence to show the game rock, paper, scissors where the winner of each game scores one point and the overall winner is the best of 21.

In most programming languages, these structures take the form if … then … else. Our game also contained repetitions: when the game was over, it started again. Another name for this is a looping structure (a list of instructions to do more than once). You write this type of program to make the computer repeat a certain command or sequence of commands. The loop may run for a predetermined number of times, until a certain condition becomes true, or as long as a certain condition remains true.

You could tell the computer to:
- Do the following 20 times.
- Do the following once for each word in the list.
- Repeat the following until the user carries out a particular action.

In this chapter we will explore this in more detail.

Why design a program first?

To program correctly, you will need to consider program design (planning) and the actual program coding. You can imagine what would happen if you built your house without first planning what you need and how it will be built.

The name given to this planning is called control structured programming.

As we have seen, there are three fundamental control structures:
- sequence
- selection
- looping (iteration).

A sequence control structure is simply a series of procedures that follow one another. A selection (if–then–else) control structure involves a choice.

Defining flow of control

Program flow control or flow of control can be defined as the order in which a program is executed or evaluated.

There are three different flow control structures, which every programming language supports. However, different programming languages may support different kinds of control flow statement.

Why it is an advantage to have structured programs?

There are several advantages when designing coded solutions in a structured manner. One is that it reduces the complexity of programming, as modularity allows the programmer to tackle problems in a logical fashion. Also, using logical structures when designing programs ensures clarity within the flow of control of the code.

Another advantage is that it increases productivity as a consequence of the modular approach, allowing a number of programmers to work on a project at the same time.

Since modules can be reused many times, it saves time and reduces complexity, as well as increasing reliability. It also offers an easier method to update or fix the program by replacing individual modules rather than larger amounts of code.

Structured programming makes extensive use of subroutines, block structures and *for* and *while* loops. This approach is in contrast to using simple tests and jumps such as using the *goto* statement that would eventually lead to something that is referred to as 'spaghetti code', that is disorganised, unstructured code which is very difficult to follow.

Structures: how things are broken down

At a basic level, structured programs comprise simple, hierarchical flow structures, which consist entirely of three types of logic structure:

- sequence
- selection
- iteration.

A sequence is where a set of instructions or actions is ordered, meaning that each action follows the previous action.

A simple sequence of actions.

Using flowcharts

There are a lot of different design procedures and techniques for building large software projects such as a new database for a large organisation. The technique discussed here, however, is for smaller coding projects and is referred to by the term 'top-down, structured flowchart methodology'.

Basic elements of flowcharts

The flowchart symbols denoting the basic building blocks of structural programming are shown in the diagram below.

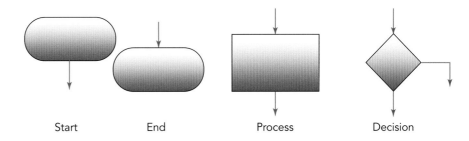

| Start | End | Process | Decision |

Flowchart symbols for start, end, process and decision.

The *start* symbol represents the start of a process, obviously. It always has exactly one output. The *start* symbol is labelled with a brief description of the process carried out by the flowchart.

The *end* symbol represents the end of a process. It always has exactly one input and generally contains either *end* or *return* depending on its function in the overall process of the flowchart.

A *process* symbol represents some operation that is carried out on an element of data. It usually contains a brief description of the process being carried out on the data. It is possible that the process could even be further broken down into simpler steps by another complete flowchart representing that process. If this is the case, the flowchart that represents the process will have the same label in the *start* symbol as the description in the process symbol at the higher level. A process always has exactly one input and one output.

A *decision* symbol always makes a Boolean choice. The label in a *decision* symbol should be a question that clearly has only two possible answers. The *decision* symbol will have exactly one input and two outputs. The two outputs will be labelled with the two answers to the question in order to show the direction of the logic flow depending on the decision made.

On-page and off-page *connectors* may also appear in some flowcharts. For the purpose of this chapter we will restrict ourselves to flowcharts that can be represented on a single page.

Using flowcharts to represent a sequence

In practice, sequences are not a simple line; usually the next action depends on the last decision. This is called selection. In selection, one statement within a set of program statements is executed depending on the state of the program at that instance.

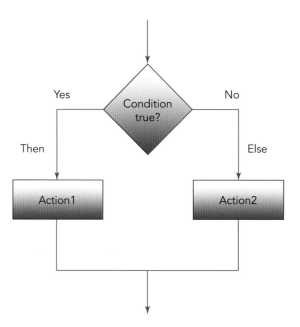

A flowchart representing selection.

Selections are usually expressed as 'decision' key words such as *if … then … else … endif, switch* or *case*. They are at the heart of all programming.

If we explore what this might look like using pseudo-code:

if condition is true
then
perform instructions in Action1
else
perform instructions in Action2
endif

Looping/iteration

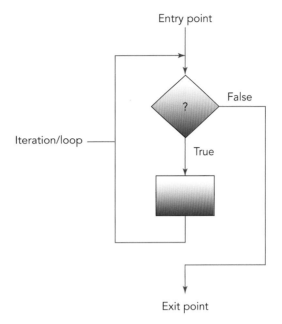

A flowchart showing an iteration/loop.

Iteration is where a statement is executed in a loop until the program reaches a certain state or the intended operations have been applied to every data element of an array. If you look at the diagram above you can see that the iteration/loop keeps on occurring until a false statement is reached.

In programming, iterations are usually expressed as 'loop' key words such as *while*, *repeat*, *for* or *do … until*. It is sometimes recommended that each iteration (loop) should have only one entry point and one exit point, and a few programming languages actually enforce this.

Task

Create a chart to show how to take a bath or shower. Start from arriving in the bathroom fully dressed and end when you are dressed again. You can start with a simple sequence but you must then add conditional loops.

Question

Complete the instructions by adding notes to the flowchart on how to play the game of snakes and ladders.

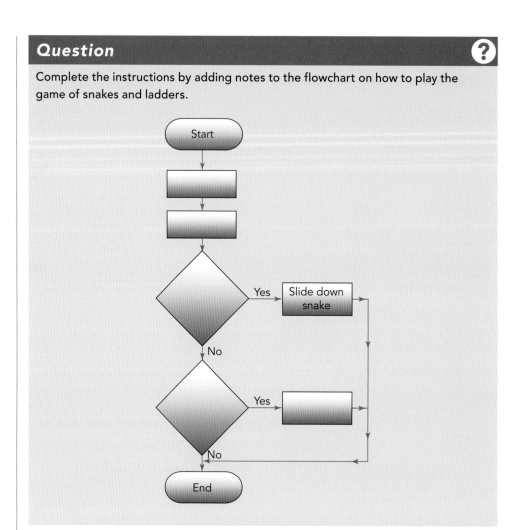

Task

Write the sequence, complete with loops and conditional statements, for the game rock, paper, scissors.

Let's look at a PHP example of an iteration:

```php
<?php
  myArray = array();
  $myArray[] = "First item";
  $myArray[] = "Second item";
  $myArray[] = "Third item";
  foreach ($myArray as $i) {
  echo "<p>$i</p>";
?>
```

You may be wondering what this bit of code does. It is called a *foreach* loop and it provides an easy way to analyse every item in an array by using a loop.

You will not only see this foreach loop in arrays. It is also possible to loop through an object. If your object contains a collection of items, you can use a foreach loop to iterate over each of them. You may see it used to loop through:

- records in a database
- navigation links
- names of files within a directory
- lines of text read from a file.

Using these building blocks

These basic building blocks are all that is needed to express any desired logic in the form of a computer program.

The very basic building block is a simple segment of straight-line code with no programming routes leaving that program statement – only one route entering it from the code that came before it.

When the syntax of a programming language encloses structures between bracketed key words such as an *if* statement or a code section bracketed by *Begin ... End,* the language is referred to as *block-structured.*

It is possible to write structured programming in any programming language; however, it is preferable to use a procedural coding language. Historically, the languages that were first used for structured programming were ALGOL, Pascal and Ada. These days, most programming languages include features that encourage a structured approach to coding and deliberately leave out other features in an attempt to prevent the language being used for unstructured coding.

Program control flowcharts

Solutions to simple programming exercises can often be designed and implemented by just sitting down and writing code. It is, however, extremely difficult to write solutions to complex problems using this approach and impossible to debug. For these reasons a structured design process is preferred. There are lots of ways of structurally designing programs, which have the following advantages:

- Allows large problems to be broken down into smaller, more manageable sections.
- Helps with testing the software.
- Helps to design programs that can easily be modified later.
- Helps to discover errors before they are programmed.
- Helps to document the solution.

Applying these structural design methods to programming makes it far more likely that the program will run successfully with the minimum amount of time and effort spent building it. This is because it increases the possibility of finding design mistakes early on in the design process. Consequently, this greatly reduces the cost of repairing the errors.

Structured design methodology also allows the modification of programs at a later date to be completed far more easily and efficiently, as these design techniques offer a much more clear and complete procedure when producing supporting documentation.

Structured designs also offer the ability for them to be broken down into natural modules, which improves testing and offers the opportunity for multiple design teams to work on areas of the project with the reassurance that the completed programs will be compatible with one another.

Top-down design

The best way to tackle the design of a program is to use top-down design. To do this you first map out the entire program and then identify the major components that it will require.

Programmers then use flowcharts and general statements to represent the logical flow of the program. Once the major components have been identified, the programmer can focus on each component in greater detail.

Basic structures

As we have already discussed, a structured flowchart is one where all of the processes and decisions must fit into one of a few basic structured elements: *sequence*, *selection* and *iteration*. The basic elements of a structured flowchart are shown in the diagram opposite. It should be possible to take any structured flowchart and enclose all of the blocks within one of the following process structures. You should make sure that you understand that each of the structures always has exactly one input and one output; therefore, a single process block can represent the structure itself.

The *sequence* process is just a series of processes that operate one after each other in a *sequence*. Most coding can be represented at the highest level by a *sequence*, often with a loop from the *end* symbol back to the *start* symbol.

The *selection* or *if … then … else* process shows a Boolean decision block as it provides two separate processes. One of the processes will be carried out in one decision path and another from the other decision path depending on the Boolean decision.

The *iteration* or *while* procedure is a representation of what is called a conditional loop within the code. This type of loop is often used in programming. The decision to run the process in the loop is made prior to the first execution of the procedure.

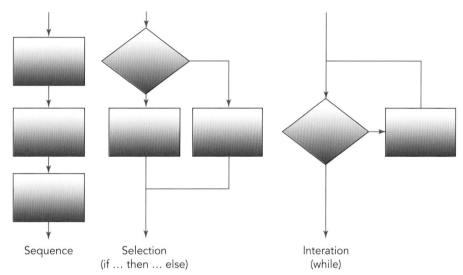

Sequence   Selection   Interation
                (if … then … else)   (while)

Sequence, selection and iteration flowcharts.

Derived structures

As has already been suggested, all flowcharts can be represented by the basic structures we have already considered. However, on occasions, it is useful to have some additional structures, each of which can itself be constructed from the basic structures. These *derived structures* are shown in the diagram below.

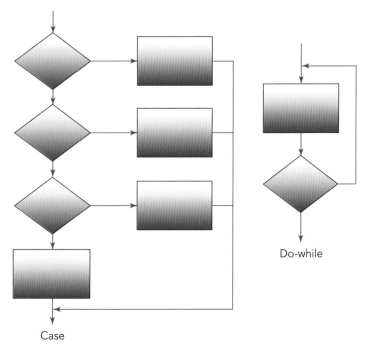

Case   Do-while

The derived structures case and do-while for use in a flowchart.

As you can see, the *do-while* structure is different from the *while* structure due to the process contained within the loop always executing at least once. This procedure is the same as if the process was performed once before going into a *while* loop. In the *while* structure it is possible that the process may never be executed. You should understand that although the *while* structure is often used, the *do-while* structure is sometimes used because it is more intuitive.

Choosing between the two is hard, so let's look at a few rules:
- Are you repeating or copying/pasting code you have already used?
- Which way uses fewer lines of code? Normally fewer is better.
- There are times when using more lines of code is more efficient, but you should never repeat yourself when coding.

Task

Produce a do-while flowchart to show how to make a breakfast of tea and toast.

Now we will look in more detail at the code.

While statements

While statements are efficient loops that will continue to loop until the condition is false. Here is the syntax:

```
while (condition) {
    // loop code here
}
```

But you must be careful. While loops can create an infinite loop and infinite loops are not a good idea in a program. Computers cannot tell if they're stuck in an infinite loop (unless you are using PHP, which has a time-out limit).

Do-while statements

Do-while statements are also efficient loops that will continue to loop until the condition is false. They are identical to while statements except that they start with do and the while condition comes after the braces. Here is the syntax:

```
do {
    // loop code here
} while (condition);
```

The difference

The difference between a while loop and a do-while loop is that in a while loop the condition is checked before the first iteration of the loop.

Here is a quick example; obviously 5 does not equal 8, so the condition is false:

```
while (5 == 8) {
  // this code will never run
}
do {
  // this code will run once
} while (5 == 8);
```

The case structure

The *case* structure is useful in showing a series of *selection* (*if ... then ... else*) procedures where there are more than two *decisions* to be made. This means that the *decision* symbols are identical except for the choice being compared. For example, the *decision* could be 'is the make of the car ... ?' Each *decision* block would then have a different make of car as the choice. One aspect of this structure that you should acknowledge is that the *true* result always flows to the right, with the *false* result flowing into the next *decision* symbol, and also there will always be one less *decision* symbol than the number of choices.

> **Key point**
>
> Structuring your program using flowcharts for each section before you enter code into a computer is essential if you want a well-designed program. If you do not do this, error checking and problem solving will take a very long time.

The diagram on the next page illustrates an example of a properly and an improperly structured flowchart. The unstructured flowchart demonstrates what can happen if a program is written first and then a flowchart is created to represent the program. As was mentioned earlier in this chapter, this type of unstructured flow is referred to as 'spaghetti code' and normally has aspects of its structure impossibly intertwined around other elements. It should be realised that a programming solution of this nature is very difficult to understand, implement, debug and maintain.

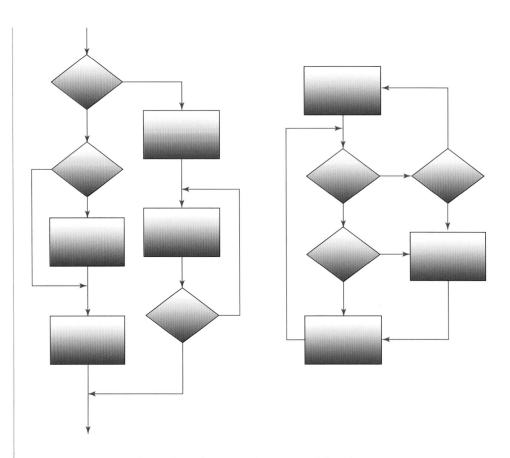

Properly and improperly structured flowcharts.

Tasks

1   Write a program flowchart for a game that does the following:
    ■ assigns the value 'outcome' to a variable called guessanswer
    ■ then assigns user input to another variable called guess1
    ■ if the user enters the value 'Computer' then the program outputs 'winner', otherwise it outputs 'incorrect' and allows the user to have another guess
    ■ permits the game to continue until the user guesses correctly.

2   Produce a structured flowchart to show how to make a cup of tea. Remember that some tasks can happen *while* other things are happening, so you should end up with a structured flowchart with decision symbols (for example, you cannot add hot water to the teabag until the kettle has boiled).

Chapter 5
Procedures and functions

Learning outcomes

- Understand what procedures and functions are in programming terms.
- Know when the use of a procedure or function would make sense and would simplify the coded solution.
- Know how to write and use your own simple procedures and functions.
- Know about and be able to describe common built-in functions in your chosen languages.
- Know how to use common built-in functions in your chosen languages when coding solutions to problems.
- Understand what a parameter is when working with procedures and functions.
- Know how to use parameters when creating efficient solutions to problems.
- Understand the concepts of parameters and return values when working with procedures and functions.

Key term

Procedures and functions are named blocks of code that can be used and reused to perform specific tasks.

Introduction

We saw in an earlier chapter that with some things, like walking, we have a set of actions that we need to be able repeat again and again. Procedures and functions are features of any programming language that allow you to repeat a certain piece of code or calculation again and again.

Procedures and functions can be called from many places in a program.

Defining procedures and functions

Procedures and functions feature in all programming languages. Their purpose is to allow the repetition of certain sections of a program or calculation many times. They also assist in the modularisation of code by allowing themselves to be called from any point within a program solution.

When to use procedures

First, let's take a closer look at procedures.

To help us, we will use a sock washing analogy. Imagine that you are a washing machine and so your process of washing socks could be:

1 Soak socks in water.
2 Cover socks with washing powder.
3 Rinse socks thoroughly.
4 Spin dry socks.

Now every time you come to wash socks, you repeat that process. Soak, washing powder, rinse, dry. Soak, washing powder, rinse, dry. Soak, washing powder, rinse, dry. A coding procedure works in the same way. Within the program the process of 'Soak, washing powder, rinse, dry' is replaced with the statement 'Wash socks', which calls that procedure.

With regard to programming, when a procedure is called, it simply does the tasks that the procedure has been assigned to do. Another important advantage with procedures is that having the capability to replace a whole load of instructions within the main body of a program with one single command makes the code considerably easier to read and debug.

> **Key term**
>
> A procedure is a block of code that performs a task without returning a value.

> **Task**
>
> Break down the task of getting ready for school into a number of separate functions. Now design a flowchart that calls up these functions at the correct time.

When to use functions

Now let's turn our attention to functions in programming.

Functions are very similar to procedures except that they return a value. This can be illustrated with an example. Say you were asked to count the number of cars in a car park. You would first enter the car park, count the cars and then report the number of cars to the person who requested the information. You have just performed a function!

In terms of programming, all a function does is simply carry out an action and then return another value back into the main program. This could be a result from a complex calculation or the number of planes that land at an airport in 24 hours or the positions of earthquakes throughout the world.

As you can see, functions can report almost anything to a main program: numbers, strings or characters. It is also worth knowing that you can use functions to replace procedures, which is particularly useful because some programming languages don't use procedures within their syntax.

Built-in functions

The real power of any programming language comes from the built-in functions. You will have already looked at these when we looked at restricted words for your chosen language. The restricted words are the built-in functions.

For example, in PHP there are more than 700 built-in functions. A function is executed by what is called 'a call' to the function. This is simply asking the function to do the task; when you counted the cars in the car park you received a call to function. If we name the action you did carpark_counting, each time someone wants you to check the number of cars in the car park they just need to give the instruction carpark_counting and you will know instantly what they want you to do.

To keep the script from being executed when the page loads, programmers put it into a function. The function is then executed by a call to the function.

When you create a function, you first need to give it a name, like writeName. It is by using this function name that you will be able to call on your function, so you should make it easy to type and understand.

The actual syntax for creating a function is easy in PHP. First, you must tell PHP that you want to create a function. You do this by typing the keyword *function* followed by your function name. Here is how you would make a function called writeName. You can call a function from anywhere within a page.

```php
<?php
  function writeName()
{
  echo "Steve";
}
  echo "My name is ";
  writeName();
?>
```

This will output:

```
My name is Steve
```

You can call a function from anywhere within a page.

You can add more functionality to a function, by adding parameters. A parameter is just like a variable. Parameters are specified after the function name, inside the parentheses.

```php
<?php
  function writeName($sname)
  {
  echo $sname . " Cushing.<br />";
  }
  echo "My name is ";
  writeName("Steve");
  echo "My sister's name is ";
  writeName("Viv");
  echo "My brother's name is ";
  writeName("Ian");
?>
```

will output:

```
My name is Steve Cushing.
My sister's name is Viv Cushing.
My brother's name is Ian Cushing
```

Tasks

1   Add a second parameter so that the output has different punctuation after each second name.

2   Find out all the functions for your chosen language.

How procedures and functions are used

So now let us have a look at how procedures and functions are written and used within a program situation.

Procedures

Procedures need to be declared. This is done using a procedure keyword, as you can see in the coding example below.

```
procedure HelloWorld;
  var
    i: integer;
  begin
    for i := 1 to 10
      Writeln('Hello World');
end;
```

In this case, the name of the procedure is the keyword *HelloWorld* and as you can see it comes first, followed by a semicolon and then the contents of the procedure.

In some respects, procedures can be viewed as mini-programs such that you declare variables and use them within your main program solution; however, after the procedure ends, the variables that it has been using disappear.

As we touched on before, the method of calling a procedure within the main program is easy. As the example below demonstrates, all you need to do is type the keyword name of the procedure within the program.

```
begin
  HelloWorld;
  Writeln('To everyone, everywhere on the planet');
end;
```

So when the program is executed and the two snippets of code above are run it will print 'Hello World' 10 times followed by the final message 'To everyone, everywhere on the planet'.

When the procedure is complete it returns to the place within the main program immediately after where the procedure was called.

Scope of variables

Now that you have a grasp of the basic concepts of procedures and functions it's time to throw the spanner in the works!

There is a catch with procedures and functions in that once they have been used within a program they are discarded along with all the variables associated with them. In other words, once you have declared a variable within procedure A, you cannot then use that same variable within procedure B – it simply disappears with the procedure once it is finished with.

Another problem related to scope is to do with namespaces. Namespaces are used to prevent two things with the same name from being confused.

Let's look at what this means using a real example. There are two people named Steve Cushing. One Steve Cushing is from Birmingham, the other is from New York.

If you want to talk about Steve Cushing, you need to indicate which one you are talking about, so you say 'Steve Cushing from Birmingham'. New York and Birmingham are called namespaces.

Question

What are namespaces and why do you need to use them in defining a variable?

Functions

Functions, however, cannot be used in the same manner as procedures because, as has been mentioned before, they return a value back to the program instead of just performing duties. An example of a function could be:

```
function AddSumValue : integer;
  begin
    AddSumValue:= x + y + z;
  end;
```

This function will return the addition of the integers *x*, *y* and *z* but how does it do that? Well, just as in the procedures, the function has a keyword name, in this case *AddSumValue*, which appears just after the command keyword 'Function'. The last item on that line is the declaration of the data type, which in this case is an integer.

The value that the function should return is assigned to the name of the function (in this case *AddSumValue*) and then returned to the main program.

Key point

A function is a block of code that has a name and a property that can be reused. It can be executed from as many different points in a program as required.

Questions

1   A programmer is developing a new program. Describe two uses of a function.
2   Give three reasons why programmers use functions.

Now let's have a look at how a function is called in the main program.

```
begin
  x := 5;
  y := 9;
  z := 4;
  Writeln(AddSumValue);
End;
```

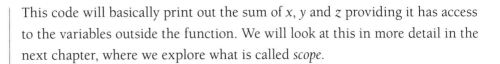

This code will basically print out the sum of *x*, *y* and *z* providing it has access to the variables outside the function. We will look at this in more detail in the next chapter, where we explore what is called *scope*.

Parameters

It has to be said that procedures and functions would have limited use if it was not for a feature called 'parameters' that allows the passing of values to the procedures and functions for use.

Let's look at a quick example:

```
function AddThem ( x, y, z: integer ) : integer;
  begin
    AddThem := x + y + z;
  end;
```

To use this function, values for *x*, *y* and *z* must be provided and this is carried out using the brackets, such that when the function is called it would read:

```
begin
   Writeln(AddThem(4, 2, 8));
end.
```

meaning that *x* would be assigned the value of 4, *y* would be assigned to 2 and *z* would be 8; in other words, passing the values over for the procedure or function to use.

Consider another quick example:

```
procedure PrintNum( x, y, z: integer );
  begin
    Writeln(x);
    Writeln(y);
    Writeln(z);
  end;
```

If the values 4, 2 and 8 were passed to this procedure, the result would be that it would basically print them out.

Chapter 6
Scope of variables, constants, functions and procedures

Specification coverage
- Scope of variables, constants, functions and procedures

Learning outcomes
- Know what is meant by the scope of a variable, constant, function or procedure.
- Be able to identify what value a particular variable will hold at a given point in the code.

Introduction

In Chapter 5 we looked at procedures and functions. In this chapter we will look at scope. Scope is an important concept in programming languages. You will not be able to read or write large computer programs without understanding the concept of scope.

The scope of something (function, variable, macro, and so on) in a program is the range of code that it applies to. Let's look at an analogy in everyday life. You have people you know at school or college and have an intranet or chat system that only people in the school can see. You may even have a special language that you use with your friends that no one outside this group would understand. This is a bit like defining a function called school with things that no one outside the school could access or understand. This is the opposite to a global social network such as Twitter, which is not restricted and anyone can see what you write.

So you have a variable that only relates to your school. This would then be called 'local-to-function' scope (local to a particular function; this would mean the variable can only be used inside the function of school). On Twitter, anyone can access what you post: it is global in both real and programming terms (usable from anywhere).

Now imagine your program as a virtual world. Parts of it will be restricted to local functions. Other parts will be global and be accessible anywhere.

In some programming languages, special things happen when variables go in and out of scope. Memory may be allocated to hold data, or memory may be freed when variables go out of scope. Scope is also useful for error checking.

The scope of a variable in a program is the lines of code in the program where the variable can be accessed. So the concept of scope applies not only to variable names but also to the names of procedures.

Defining what is meant by 'scope'

When we talk about how variables may be accessed and how procedures may be called, what we are actually talking about is referred to as scope. A variable can be declared in a number of ways:

- When it is only accessible to a single procedure.
- When it is accessible to all procedures within a module, and so on up the hierarchy of a project or group of related projects.

There is another term that is used to describe scope and that is *visibility*. You should be aware that the two terms are the same in programming and that there are four 'levels' of scope:

- procedure scope
- module scope
- project scope
- global scope.

Procedure scope

The term *procedure scope* refers to when a variable can be read and modified *only* from within the procedure in which it is declared. It cannot be accessed from another project or even from another module in the same project.

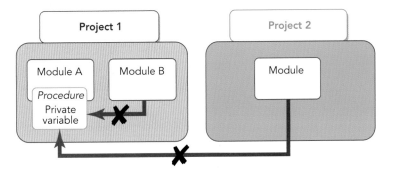

Let's take a look at the Visual Basic example below:

```
Sub TestRoutine()
  Dim X As Long
  Dim Y As Long
  X = 1234
  Y = 4321
  Debug.Print "X: " & X, "Y: " & Y
End Sub
```

In the above example, the variables (*X* and *Y*) can only be accessed within the TestRoutine procedure. The variables are created when TestRoutine is called and they are destroyed when TestRoutine ends. It should be understood that these variables cannot be accessed or modified from any other procedure. *Procedure scope* has the highest priority with regard to the other scope levels. So, in addition to these variables, if you have variables with the same names declared at a *module scope* level (see next section), the code within the TestRoutine procedure uses the variables declared within this procedure, not the variables with the same name declared at the module level.

```php
<?PHP
function display_error_message(){
  $error_text = "Error message";
  print $error_text;
}
display_error_message();
?>
```

Notice how the variable called $error_text is inside the function. If you don't do this you will get a PHP error!

Module scope

This term refers to when a variable is declared before and outside of any procedure within a project. In Visual Basic, if you use the keywords Private or Dim to declare variables, only procedures that are in the same module can read and modify that variable. As a consequence of module-level variables not being part of any specific procedure, they retain their values even after the procedure responsible for altering their values has been destroyed. It is sometimes called a friendly global variable as it can be accessed by any procedure of any module of the same project. A procedure of another project cannot access that variable.

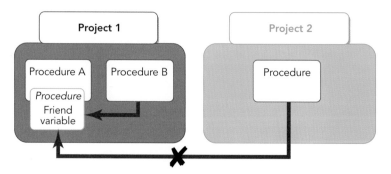

Let's analyse the following statement:

```
Dim MVar As Long
```

In this statement, the variable MVar can be accessed from any procedure in the same module as the declaration. However, it cannot be read or modified from a procedure that is contained within another module.

You should understand that different modules could declare variables with the same name. For instance, both Module A and Module B could have a module-level variable named MVar. Each module-level variable will be read or modified by procedures within the same module.

Now, if both Module A and Module B have a module-level variable named MVar, procedures within Module A will access the variable MVar defined within Module A and procedures within Module B will access the variable MVar defined in Module B. So you can see that variables with the same name in different modules are completely independent of one another, even though they have the same name.

With regard to Visual Basic statements, you can use either Dim or Private to declare a module-level variable that can only be read and modified within that module. To illustrate this fact look at the two statements below – they are basically functionally equivalent:

```
Dim MVar As Long
Private MVar As Long
```

Task

Research the types of scope available in your chosen programming language.

Question

Describe two kinds of scope used in programming.

Project scope

This level of variable is declared using the public command keyword and it can be read and modified from any procedure contained within any module within the program or *project*.

You should be aware that you cannot declare a *project scope* variable if it has not got global scope. As we saw in the diagrams earlier, to ensure that a variable is accessible from anywhere across projects you must use the public command. Remember, the scope of a variable refers to the areas of code that a variable is visible in.

Various programming languages have various different scoping rules for the different kinds of declarations we have considered, so you will need to explore

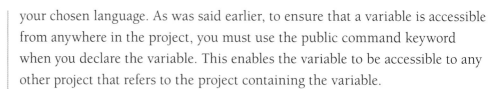

your chosen language. As was said earlier, to ensure that a variable is accessible from anywhere in the project, you must use the public command keyword when you declare the variable. This enables the variable to be accessible to any other project that refers to the project containing the variable.

Normally, all variables declared using the public statement are available to all procedures in all modules in all projects unless your programming language has what is called an Option Private Module. In this case, variables are public only within the project in which they reside and therefore have only module scope.

Global scope

The final level of variables are called *global scope* variables. These variables have the capability of being accessed from anywhere within the *project* that contains their declaration as well as from other *projects* that refer to that initial *project*. Because it can also be read by other projects, it is often said to be *public*. A *public* global variable can be accessed by any procedure of its project and procedures of other projects.

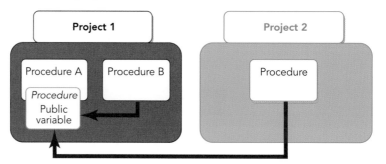

In order to declare a *global scope* variable, you use the public keyword within a module that does not contain the Option Private Module directive. To access variables within another *project*, you simply use the variable's name. Care should be taken though if it is believed that the calling project also contains a variable of the same name. If this is the case, then you need to add the project name to the variable's name so it is clear where it is from. Let's illustrate this with an example.

If you have a Project A that declares a variable as AnyVarib and Project B refers to Project A, then the code within Project B has the capability to read and modify AnyVarib with either of the following statements:

```
AnyVarib = 1234
Project1.AnyVarib = 1234
```

Now, if both Project A and B contain variables of at least *project scope* level, you will need to include the project name along with the variable.

As has been stated earlier, when coding it is common practice to include the project name, especially when reading or modifying a variable that is declared within another project. This makes it much easier to understand what is happening when looking at the code.

Scope and procedures

The procedures with the keywords Sub, Function and Property are similar to variables in that they also follow the rules of scope. However, that is where the similarity ends as they differ with regard to their implementation.

As we have considered earlier, any procedure that has been declared within the module can be used within another procedure that exists in the same coding project providing the procedure uses the private keyword. Also, if we use the public declaration, it is the same as leaving out the scope declaration entirely.

This is all quite complex, so let's try to simplify it with an example showing how procedures can be called from any other procedure in any other module of the project:

```
Public Sub TheProcedureName()
    Debug.Print "The Procedure Name"
End Sub
```

```
Sub TheProcedureName()
    Debug.Print "The Procedure Name"
End Sub
```

In order to write a procedure that can only be accessed from within the module that it is contained in, you must use the private declaration, as shown below:

```
Private Sub TheRoutine()
    Debug.Print "HelloWorld"
End Sub
```

Just as in variables, the public keyword gives the procedure the ability to be accessed by all procedures contained within the project along with procedures within other projects that refer to the initial procedure.

In order to make the procedure accessible from all parts of the host project, but not from other projects, you can use the Option Private Module directive. As with variables, this ensures that only procedures within the same project can access the initial procedure. So, procedures that you wish to be accessible to other projects should be placed in a module that does not include the Option Private Module directive, but it should be included in all other modules.

In PHP, the scope of a variable is controlled by the location of the variable's declaration. This determines the parts of the program that can access it.

There are four types of variable scope in PHP: local, global, static and function parameters.

Local scope in PHP

Local scope is where a variable is declared in a function. It is not accessible outside the function.

In addition, by default, variables defined outside a function (called global variables) are not accessible inside the function. For example:

```
function update_counter1 () {
  $counter1++;
}
$counter1 = 100;
update_counter1();
echo $counter1;
100
```

The $counter1 inside the function is local to that function.

Only functions can provide local scope. Unlike in other languages, in PHP you cannot create a variable whose scope is a loop.

Global scope in PHP

Variables declared outside a function are global. They can be accessed from any part of the program. However, they are not available inside functions. To allow a function to access a global variable, you must use the global keyword inside the function to declare the variable. Let's look at the code and see how it differs:

```
function update_counter1 () {
  global $counter1;
  $counter1++;
}
$counter1 = 100;
update_counter1();
echo $counter1;
```

Tasks

1 Write a short piece of code in your chosen language that includes a scope statement.

2 See if you can work out what the following code will do:

```
function roll () {
    return mt_rand(1,6);
}
```

```
echo roll();
```

Complete the code in your chosen programming language.

Chapter 7
Error handling

Specification coverage

- The different types of error that can occur
- How to test your code for errors
- How to detect errors from within code
- How to recover from errors within the code

Learning outcomes

- You should be able to discuss and identify the different types of errors that can occur within code (syntax, run-time and logical).
- Understand that some errors can be detected and corrected during the coding stage.
- Understand that some errors will occur during the execution of the code.
- Know how to detect errors at execution time and how to handle those errors to prevent your program from crashing where desirable.
- You should be able to use trace tables to check your code for errors.
- Understand that computer programs can be developed with tools to help the programmer detect and deal with errors (for example, watch, breakpoint and step).

Introduction

However hard you try to avoid errors they are inevitable in any program. Even if you coded your program perfectly, the users of your program will always discover some problem in your application that you never even dreamed possible.

Although it's impossible to eliminate every error, this chapter describes errors and should help you to avoid most coding errors.

Different types of error in computer programming

There are basically three types of error that computer programmers encounter when writing software. These are:

- syntax errors
- run-time errors
- logic errors.

> **Key point**
>
> If you write 12 or more lines of code expect to find a syntax error, a bad array reference or a misspelled variable. This is quite normal.

Syntax errors

Syntax errors, or as they are sometimes known, format errors, are a big problem for those who are new to programming. A syntax error occurs when the programmer fails to obey, usually through inexperience, one of the grammar rules of the programming language that they are using to write an application. Typically, this might be down to using the wrong case, placing punctuation in positions where it should not exist or failing to insert punctuation where it should be placed within the code.

Some programming languages are specifically designed to help new programmers use a 'drag and drop' method of writing code. This is where the user clicks and drags snippets of code into the place in the program where they are required. This allows them the freedom to concentrate on creating a solution to a programming problem with a robust structure without having the added distraction of satisfying syntax requirements.

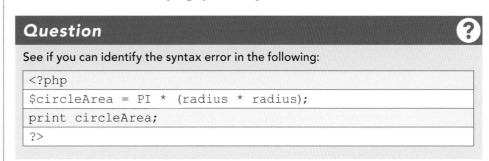

> **Question** ❓
>
> See if you can identify the syntax error in the following:
>
> ```php
> <?php
> $circleArea = PI * (radius * radius);
> print circleArea;
> ?>
> ```

Run-time errors

Run-time errors occur whenever the program instructs the computer to carry out an operation that it is either not designed to do or slow to do. As a consequence of the huge number of situations that can be categorised within this area, there is equally a huge number of ways to write programs that cause run-time errors.

In some programs, run-time errors commonly occur when programming statements are written in the wrong order or a programmer constructs instructions that the computer is unable to carry out.

One of the commonest run-time errors is when a program instructs a computer to divide any number by the value of zero. This operation produces an infinitely large result, which is too large for a computer to accommodate. In this situation, the computer will return an error message informing the user that it is unable to perform that operation.

> **Question**
>
> Explain the term run-time error.

Logic errors

Out of the three common errors that occur in programming, logic errors are typically the most difficult kind of errors to detect and rectify. This is usually because there is no obvious indication of the error within the software. The program will run successfully; however, it will not behave in the manner it was designed to. In other words it will simply produce incorrect results.

The most common reasons for logic errors are usually a consequence of one of the following:
- The programmer did not understand the manner in which the program was meant to behave.
- The programmer did not understand the individual behaviour of each operation that was part of the program.
- Careless programming.

It is worth noting that often logic errors can remain undetected until an angry user contacts the programmer to say that their program has performed some calamitous operation such as paying all the employees of a company too much in their monthly salary!

So, how can logic errors be prevented? Well, the following rules should prevent most of the errors occurring:
- Programmers should fully understand how a finished program is meant to behave.
- Programmers should have a thorough knowledge of the behaviour of every operation that is written into the program.
- Careless programming must be avoided.
- A thorough and rigorous testing strategy should be implemented.

> **Question**
>
> A programmer is developing a new program. Describe the types of errors they would check for.

Testing for errors before and during the coding stages

It is important to thoroughly test a system in order to ensure that it is robust and not likely to malfunction. It should be understood, however, that a program is very unlikely to work perfectly the first time it is executed. Therefore testing is carried out on the code to try and make it fail and reveal the presence of errors. If software is not tested effectively the consequences could be:

- The reputation of the company that has written the program could be ruined.
- An accident could be caused if the code is part of a program that runs a system, for example, on an aircraft or in a nuclear power station.

In the next section we will look at debugging, which is the process of detecting and correcting errors during execution of the program. However, next we will look at how errors can be detected prior to running the program.

Dry-run testing

Dry-run testing is usually carried out on the algorithm which is written in pseudo-code or as part of a flowchart. This form of testing is usually done prior to the program code being written.

The process involves stepping through the algorithm one instruction at a time with purposely chosen example test data. A 'trace table' is used by the programmer to keep track of the test data, its purpose being to demonstrate what went wrong within an algorithm and pinpoint exactly where the problem is. It should be understood that this form of testing is usually done on a small scale as it is quite hard work and very repetitive.

The main advantage of dry-run testing is that it enables programmers to spot errors even before they start writing code.

Proving code correctness using unit testing

If a programmer has only to check the correctness of the code within a small program, they may just go literally go through the program line by line checking for errors manually. Now, this is tedious enough with a small program and is also open to human error, so you can imagine that with large programs this process of proving code correctness is completely unfeasible. Professional program developers use software tools called unit tests.

Unit testing is a popular practice that consists of writing additional programs that test individual functions of a main program under development. Unit tests are small pieces of code whose purpose is to prove the correctness of aspects such as methods of software modules.

Unit testing is an important process as it is an automatic tool that can uncover 'regressions'. These are unwanted changes in previously working code which may have inadvertently been introduced during development.

Like other software, there are effective and ineffective unit tests. A poor unit test will focus on a scenario that is not relevant for the application, while a good-quality unit test is one that is written to catch cases such as a scenario where someone enters a negative value as a salary figure.

'Code coverage' is a term that is used to describe the percentage of lines of code that are covered by unit tests. It should be realised, however, that there is no relationship between the number of unit tests applied to a program and the potential correctness of the code.

Testing for errors during the execution of code

The process of testing a program for errors during its execution is a cyclic activity called *debugging*. To debug code effectively, two things are needed:

- the ability to test each of the instructions provided by a program, and
- the ability to retrieve the information about:
  - the results of those instructions
  - any changes in the program when the tests were carried out
  - the error conditions
  - what the program was doing when the error occurred.

Fortunately, there are software tools that can assist in the debugging process. These tools are called *debuggers* and the source code of a program is run through these in order to detect syntax, run-time and logic errors. The debugger produces a report that highlights and lists the above information to the program tester.

There are a number of specific features within debuggers that can assist the program tester in detecting errors, such as:

- breakpoints
- steps
- watches.

Breakpoints

Breakpoints are breaks that can be inserted manually into code by the tester in order to halt the execution of the program at specific points. This allows the tester to inspect the code at those points. Usually, code on the line where a breakpoint has been inserted will be highlighted in a red or yellow colour. Any number of breakpoints can be inserted into a program, although a limit is reached when there really is no reason to insert any more breakpoints.

Steps

Once the program is paused (say by a breakpoint), the debugger allows the tester to continue the execution of the program one line at a time – effectively stepping through the program. This allows a programmer to see exactly how many variables and objects are affected when a particular line is executed.

Watches

Watches are usually in the format of a table and display the values of specified fields and variables relative to the particular line that the debugger is currently on. To add a watch, the tester usually types the name of the variable that they are interested in within an area of the user interface of the debugging program.

Also, expressions that require evaluation, such as $x + 1$ or array accesses, can be typed in to a watch.

Trace tables

A trace table is a technique used to test algorithms to see if any logic errors occur while the algorithm is being processed.

Within the table, each column contains a variable and each row displays each numerical input into the algorithm and the resultant values of the variables.

Trace tables are particularly popular with people who are learning to program.

How to create a trace table

Remember that an algorithm is simply a sequence or series of steps. You can 'freeze' the algorithm on paper at any point and take a virtual snapshot of the state of all the variables.

A trace table is a very useful tool that allows you to see the state of your algorithm with as much detail as you wish.

Step	Now	Last	Count
1			
2			
3			

All you need to do is to create a table in which each row shows the state of the step in the algorithm and each column shows the value of a variable at that step. In the example above, we have three variables, *now*, *last* and *step*, and we are showing three steps in the program sequence. You would simply add the data in the variables for each step.

Question

Describe three methods that a programmer can deploy to test for errors when programming.

Chapter 8
Handling external data

Specification coverage
- How to use text files to read/write data
- How to use databases to read/write data

Learning outcomes
- You should know how to use an external text file to read and write data in a way that is appropriate for the programming languages used and the problem being solved.
- You should know how to read and write data from an external database in a way that is appropriate for the programming languages used and the problem being solved.

Introduction

Up until now we have held all the data we need inside the program using arrays. Sometimes we need much more data and this has to be held externally, which means outside the program itself. One example of this could be a dictionary. There would be far too much data in a dictionary to be held in an array. This chapter looks at ways that a programmer could use external data within a program or routine.

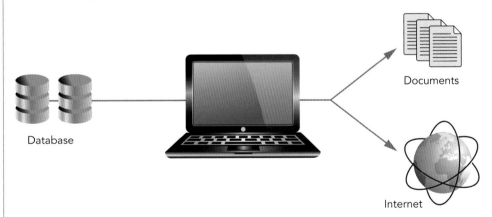

Database

Documents

Internet

Data held in an external database can be collected, analysed and passed on.

Using text files to read and write data

Text files are a popular and convenient format that allows programs, created in a range of different languages, to handle external data. They offer a common denominator format that can be understood by both people and computers.

They also provide a method of reading data from and writing data to software applications.

The following sequence highlights the basic steps, within most programs and languages, to work with text files:

1 Open the text file.
2 Read from or write to the text file.
3 Close the file.

Key point

All programs have to deal with external data. Imagine a program that produces no output and accepts no input. Such a program would be of no use. All programs either accept data from sources outside the coding of the program, or will produce some kind of output. Often they do both.

Writing to a text file

When you write information to a text file, you are adding data to that file. We can use PHP to write to a text file. The *fwrite* function in PHP allows data to be written to any type of file.

The fwrite function's first parameter is the file handle and its second is the string of data that is to be written. You only have to give the fwrite function these two pieces of information. Let's take a look at this in code:

```php
<?PHP
  $myFile = "testFile.txt";
  $handle = fopen($myFile, 'w') or die("can't open file");
  $stringData = "Steve Cushing\n";
  fwrite($handle, $stringData);
  $stringData = "Ian Cushing\n";
  fwrite($handle, $stringData);
  fclose($handle);
?>
```

This will create a text file containing Steve Cushing and my brother Ian Cushing. So what happens if I want to add more data to my existing text file? If I write:

```php
<?PHP
  $myFile = "testFile.txt";
  $handle = fopen($myFile, 'w') or die("can't open file");
  $stringData = "Cerri Cushing\n";
  fwrite($handle, $stringData);
  $stringData = "Xian Cushing\n";
  fwrite($handle, $stringData);
  fclose($fhandle);
?>
```

all the existing data contained in the file will be wiped clean and I will start with an empty file. In this example we open our existing file *testFile.txt* and write some new data into it: Cerri Cushing and Xian Cushing.

The program creates a text file when it runs. Within the contents of the directory, where the executable program would be located, there would be a text file given a name. If I want to hold the text file in another location I have to define the location.

```php
<?php
$handle = fopen("c:\\folder\\testFile.txt", "r");
?>
```

So what does the 'r' do?

r'	Open for read only
rb	You can use the 'b' command to force to binary
a'	Open for writing only; place the file pointer at the end of the file
a+'	Open for reading and writing; place the file pointer at the end of the file
x'	Create and open for writing only; place the file pointer at the beginning of the file
x+'	Create and open for reading and writing; otherwise it has the same behaviour as 'x'
c'	Open the file for writing only. If the file does not exist, it is created
w	Open for writing only

Reading from a text file

Before we can read information from a file we have to use a function to open it. In PHP this is the *fopen* function.

```php
$myFile = "testFile.txt";
$handle = fopen($myFile, 'r');
```

In PHP, the *fread* function is the normal way to get data out of a file. The function requires a file handle and an integer to tell the function how much data, in bytes, we want to extract. One character is equal to one byte. If you want to read the first four characters then you would use 4 as the integer.

```php
<?PHP
  $myFile = "testFile.txt";
  $handle = fopen($myFile, 'r');
  $theData = fread($handle, 4);
  fclose($handle);
  echo $theData;
?>
```

This would output Cerr from our text file as we defined 4 bytes, as you can see we have used the 'r' as we only want to read the data. The most common use of this function is to place lines of text into an array.

Let's look at an example of this using the *explode()* string function to create an array from each line of text.

```
<?PHP

$file_handle = fopen("dictionary.txt", "rb");

while (!feof($file_handle) ) {

$line_of_text = fgets($file_handle);
$part = explode('=', $line_of_text);

print $part[0] . $part[1]. "<BR>";
}

fclose($file_handle);

?>
```

You will recognise most of the code. The first line to explore is this:

```
$part = explode('=', $line_of_text);
```

The explode function splits a line of text, based on whatever you have provided for the separator. In this piece of code, the equals sign (=) is the separator. This is because each line in the dictionary.txt file looks like this:

```
LOL = Laughing Out Loud
```

When the explode function is executed, the variable called $part will be an array. We then print out both parts of the array with this:

```
print $part[0] . $part[1]. "<BR>";
```

So $part[0] will hold the abbreviation (LOL) and $part[1] will hold the meaning Laughing Out Loud.

Question

A programmer is developing an online computer game. Describe the types of data they might store in a string rather than externally.

Reading and writing data from external databases

Reading and writing from a text document and holding data in a data string works fine for a large number of applications. But what happens when you need to store and retrieve large amounts of data? For example, in a web-based membership scheme or a game that stores the scores of all the players, your program has to talk to a database.

There are many situations when a programmer may wish to split the program from the rest of the data; for example, to ease the issues of distributing the program where all of the instances of the application can access one external database for information. One of the most common ways of doing this is to use Structured Query Language, or SQL as it is usually called. SQL is used to communicate with a database. SQL has become the standard language for relational database management systems.

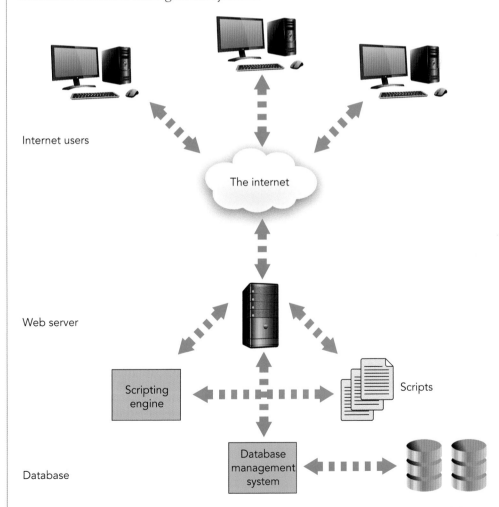

A possible use for SQL. Internet users access the website from the web server and the scripting engine accesses the database.

As can be seen in the diagram, users on the internet can access the website from the web server and the scripting engine (SQL) accesses the database.

SQL statements are used to perform tasks such as update data on a database, or retrieve data from a database.

Key point

Although SQL is an ANSI (American National Standards Institute) standard, there are many different versions of the SQL language; however, they all support the following commands: SELECT, UPDATE, DELETE, INSERT, WHERE.

Some of the common relational database management systems that use SQL include Oracle, Sybase, Microsoft SQL Server, Access and Ingres.

Standard SQL commands such as 'Select', 'Insert', 'Update', 'Delete', 'Create' and 'Drop' can be used to accomplish almost everything that a programmer needs to do with a database.

PHP has support for over 20 databases, including all of the most popular commercial and open-source databases. Relational database systems such as MySQL and Oracle are the backbone of most modern, dynamic websites. They are used for things like shopping-cart information, customer purchase records and histories, product reviews, user and membership information, credit-card numbers, and sometimes even web pages themselves.

Whatever programming language you use, you will need to also use a relational database management system (RDBMS). This is a server that manages data for you. The data is structured into tables, where each table has a number of columns, each of which has a name and a type. For example, to keep track of computer science books, we could create a 'books' table that records the book's title (as a string), year of publication (as a number) and the author's name (as a string).

Tables would then be grouped together into the databases, so a computer science book database might have tables for authors, titles and programming languages.

PHP communicates with relational databases such as MySQL and Oracle using SQL. You can use SQL to create, modify and query relational databases.

Question

A programmer is developing an online computer game. What are the benefits and drawbacks of using a text file to store the data?

As a programming example in SQL, let us go back to our book database. To search only for the books published in the year 2012 you would use:

```
SELECT * FROM books WHERE pub_year = 2012
```

You can issue queries that bring together information from multiple tables. For example, this query joins together the book and author tables to let you see who wrote each book:

```
SELECT author.name, books.title FROM books, author
WHERE author.author = books.author.
```

We can delete all the books published in 2012 from the database using:

```
DELETE FROM books WHERE pub_year = 2012
```

or insert into the database using:

```
INSERT INTO books (title, author, ISBN, pub_year) VALUES
(Computer Science, 'Steve, Cushing, '978-1444-18226-2', 2013)
```

To update a record to change a publication date use this SQL statement:

```
UPDATE books SET pub_year=2013 WHERE author="Steve Cushing"
```

Questions

1 A programmer is developing an online computer game. What are the benefits of using SQL?

2 Write an SQL statement to add the following data to the books' table:
ICT, 'Steve, Cushing', 978-0719-57264-7, 2011.

Chapter 9
Systems

Specification coverage
- The definition of a 'system'
- The importance of computer systems to the modern world
- The importance of reliability and robustness of computer systems

Learning outcomes
- You should be able to define a computer system.
- Understand and be able to discuss the importance of computer systems to the modern world.
- Understand that computer systems must be reliable and robust and be able to discuss the reasons why this is important.

Introduction

So far in this book we have looked at programs and how they are coded. But a program is of no use without a computer system to run it on. There are a vast number of different types of computer systems but they all have a number of common elements.

In this chapter of the book we will look at the basic parts that make up a computer system.

Definition of a computer system

In its very basic form, a computer system can be looked at as nothing more than the following:
- input
- processing
- storage
- output.

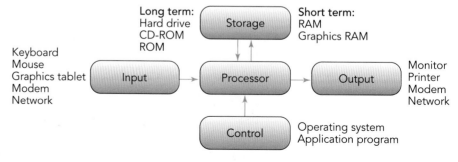

The definition of a computer system.

As the simple diagram shows, a computer system will also be equipped with some storage capability. For processing to take place, the system requires instructions for the processing that is needed to be carried out in the form of a program.

A computer system will also need to communicate with other technological devices such as phones, tablet computers, games consoles and so on.

Input

The input of a computer system is usually provided by hardware devices in the form of digital data or commands. Examples of these devices include:

- keyboard
- mouse
- scanner
- microphone.

Computer input devices. How many do you use?

Key point

You need to think very carefully about input devices. Normally a monitor is not an input device. But if it is a touchscreen as supplied on most smartphones it is an input and an output device. Similarly, new printers can send signals back to the computer when they run out of ink or paper.

Processing

The processing is carried out by a range of hardware, such as the actual processor on the motherboard, a graphics card or a soundcard, and software, such as the applications, utility programs and the operating system.

Storage

Data input into a computer has to be stored somewhere. Data is stored in a computer on some sort of data storage medium usually called memory. This will be covered in more detail in Chapter 10.

Output

Hardware devices also provide the output from a computer system. This is where the processed information is presented to the user in a readable and usable form. Devices that do this include:

- monitors
- speakers
- printers.

Computer output devices. How many do you use?

Question

Describe three common devices that are both input and output devices.

Even when you press the 'on' button to start your computer you are providing input. The system software then instructs the CPU (central processing unit) to start up certain programs and to switch on some of the hardware devices to ensure that they are ready to receive more input from you. This whole process is called 'booting up'.

The next step occurs when you select an application (program) you wish to use.

You provide further input by clicking on the icon or entering a command to start the program. Let's use a web browser as an example. Once the program has loaded and is on the screen it is ready for your instructions. You enter an address and press return and the computer immediately knows what you want it to do. The browser software then searches the internet for that address, starting up other hardware devices, such as a modem, when it requires them. Once it has found the correct address, the browser informs your computer to send the information from the web page over the phone line to your computer and eventually, you see the website you were looking for on your screen.

The importance of computer systems to the modern world

As time moves on, computer systems will probably become even more integral to our everyday lives. Think about all of the computer systems that we use regularly now, such as:

- washing/drying programs on washing machines
- the computers that monitor and control systems and facilities within cars
- the cashless catering systems that a lot of schools use
- voice-activated smartphones
- self-service supermarket checkouts that scan, weigh, process payment and give change
- contactless payment systems that use RFID (radio frequency identification) tags in credit and debit cards that are read when a card is placed near a reader
- RFID technology in library books and in products in shops to detect if the item is being removed without authorisation. This technology is also being used in clothing that communicates with washing machines and informs the machines how to wash the garment.

Key point
Computer chips control many of the products we use each day.

In the world of business, people rely on computer systems to help them to do their jobs easily and more efficiently. Computer systems allow business people to create business documentation that is error free and professional in appearance.

Computer systems allow people to work together on projects. Whether they are in the next office or on opposite sides of the world, they can edit and share documents easily and collaborate on the production of documentation, drawings or reports.

Even calendars can be shared between colleagues so that meetings can be booked with the confidence that they don't clash with other appointments.

With the improvements in technology, working from home or 'teleworking' has become increasingly popular. People can even securely log into their company's network via the internet, work on files, share them with fellow workers and use the organisation's intranet.

Large global organisations such as banks use computer systems to provide the following:
- secure access to customer accounts
- online banking
- cash machines.

Entertainment organisations use computer systems for:
- online booking services
- WiFi-connected computers and printers to issue tickets on a customer's arrival.

Schools use computer systems for:
- learning environments and for the storage of students' work
- attendance and registration systems, sometimes even using a biometric system of registering
- cashless money systems for the dining hall.

Take a moment to think back to five years ago and ask yourself how much of the above technology existed. Think how computers have changed the way we live with the technological advances in communication, shopping, entertainment, banking, travel and even how your lessons are delivered in school.

Computer systems are now all around us. Instead of being things that we use now and again, if we want to, they have now become part of our everyday lives with regard to the services they provide and the data that they hold. In many ways their importance has increased so much that they are no longer just a luxury, they have become a necessity for modern living.

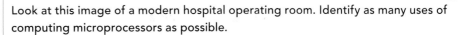

Task

Look at this image of a modern hospital operating room. Identify as many uses of computing microprocessors as possible.

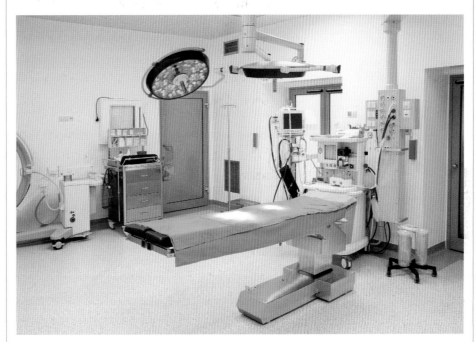

A modern operating theatre in a hospital.

The need for reliability in modern computer systems

As we have looked at earlier, in these modern technological times we have come to depend on computer systems a great deal, taking advantage of the services that they offer and the data that they can store. You can then understand that excellent reliability in computer systems is very important.

What is reliability?

When someone can be depended on to do something we want them to do, we call them reliable. Computer systems are similar; however, the advantage with them is that reliability can be measured.

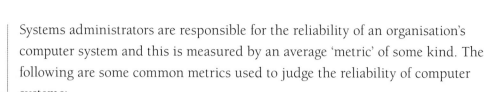

Systems administrators are responsible for the reliability of an organisation's computer system and this is measured by an average 'metric' of some kind. The following are some common metrics used to judge the reliability of computer systems:

- AVAIL. This uses the percentage of time that a system is available to users but ignoring any planned maintenance periods when the system is down.
- MTTF. This stands for 'mean time to failure' and is the average number of hours that a system operates for before it malfunctions. This metric tends to be most commonly applied to hardware such as servers.

The consequences of failure

Malfunctions of systems can be catastrophic for both organisations and people.

Just imagine if your computer's hard disk failed right at this moment! What impact would this have on you? What if it held all of your GCSE work for every subject or your whole music collection? You should have some sort of back-up system just in case this happens.

What if an organisation that provides telephone and broadband services had a fire in its data centre and the equipment holding its customer accounts went up in flames? It makes sense for the company to have in place plans and strategies for disaster recovery.

Question

Explain three instances in everyday objects that you will personally use where time between failures could be critical.

Redundancy

It is a fact of life that systems will eventually break down and so there is a need to put strategies in place to deal with this. With regard to computer systems the method that is used is called 'redundancy'.

Redundancy is a method of breakdown prevention where important parts of a system are duplicated so that in the event of a failure the other components can take their place.

Data redundancy

This is a strategy where important data is duplicated in a number of places within the computer system so that if one area of the system breaks down or becomes corrupted, the data will not be lost. An example of this is running two hard disk drives in parallel, where they both store the same data.

Software redundancy

This is a less common strategy that tends to be used for safety-critical applications. The purpose for software redundancy is that it is very difficult to create programs that don't contain any bugs at all, and in the event of a bizarre fault an undetected bug may have disastrous consequences.

Therefore, for critical software where failure cannot happen, there will be three software routines in place – each written by independent programming teams – each producing the same output when the same input is applied. These systems tend to be used in places such as:

- aircraft
- medical equipment
- railway safety controls
- nuclear power stations.

Question

Explain two different types of redundancy in computing.

Backing up

As well as redundancy, organisations use a strategy where data is stored in other locations. This is called backing up data.

For individuals who perhaps run a small office, it is important to attach an external hard drive and a good back-up program to each personal computer they use.

For organisations using network servers, the common practice is to use digital tape machines to replicate data on a remote server.

Large organisations may even duplicate a whole data centre in a separate location so that in the event of a fire no data will be lost.

Recently, individuals and organisations have begun to contract external companies who specialise in data storage. The businesses and individuals upload their data to a remote data centre, which is maintained and managed by the specialist company.

This is part of the cloud computing system that was discussed in the first chapter and is increasing in popularity as a cost-effective back-up solution for businesses and individuals. Some modern software even backs up the data to remote cloud-based servers automatically, sometimes every few seconds.

But cloud computing offers more than just backing up and shared documents. Cloud computing lets users access all their applications and documents from anywhere in the world.

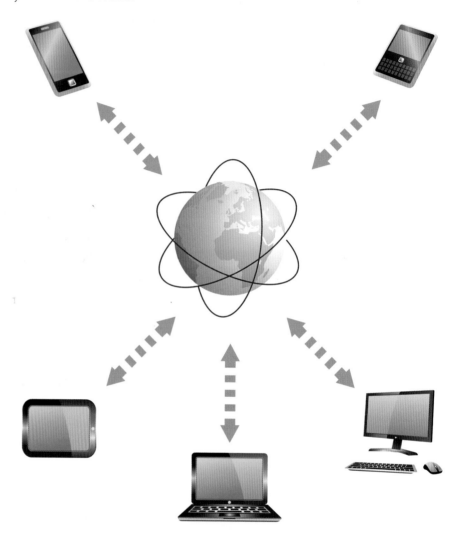

Backing up. Can you think of a way of doing this using the internet?

Question

List five criteria that you would need to consider in developing a policy for backing up your data.

Cloud computing has led to a major change in how we back up data, store information and run applications. Instead of installing applications (often referred to as apps) on individual computers, everything can be hosted in the cloud. But as with all computing there are advantages and disadvantages of cloud computing.

Advantages of cloud computing

- *Automatic back-up.* On a computer, a hard disk crash can destroy all your valuable data if it is stored on the device, but if it is in the cloud a computer crash shouldn't affect any of your data.
- *Device independence.* You are not limited to working on a document stored on a single computer or network. You can change computer and even change to your mobile device, and the documents follow you through the cloud.
- *Improved compatibility.* You don't have to worry about the documents you create on your machine being compatible with your other devices; there are no format incompatibilities when everyone is sharing docs and apps in the cloud.
- *Improved performance.* With fewer programs using the computer's memory, you get better performance from your computing system.
- *Instant software updates.* Cloud-based software is always up to date.
- *Lower computer/device costs.* You do not need an expensive computer to run cloud computing's web-based applications. Applications run in the cloud, so they do not need the processing power or hard disk space that you would need for locally installed software. Your computing device requires a smaller hard disk and less memory. This has helped to enable the growth in mobile devices with small solid-state hardware.
- *Reduced software costs.* Instead of purchasing expensive software applications, you can get most of what you need online at a much lower cost or even free.
- *Universal access.* You don't carry your files and documents with you; they stay in the cloud, and you access them whenever you have a computer or mobile and an internet connection. All your documents are instantly available wherever you are.
- *Unlimited storage capacity.* Cloud computing offers limitless storage, in theory.

Disadvantages of cloud computing

- *Can be slower.* Even on a very fast connection, web-based applications can sometimes be slower than accessing a similar software program on a desktop or laptop computer.
- *Cloud computing will not work as well with low-speed connections.* Web-based apps and large documents and images require a lot of bandwidth.
- *Cloud computing requires a reliable internet connection.* Cloud computing is impossible if you cannot connect to the internet.
- *Limited features.* Many web-based applications do not have as many features as conventional computer programs, but this is changing and some new apps have enhanced features.
- *Security.* As all your data is stored on the cloud, it is more vulnerable.

Given the many advantages, companies such as Apple, Google and Microsoft have all developed cloud-based software and data services.

A growing number of people want to access the latest version of their documents on a range of different devices. The benefits of shared documents in business, where a number of people work together on a single project, are driving this cloud-based technology forward even faster. This has also led to changes in computer programming, with web-based computer languages such as PHP, HTML5 and Java becoming more and more popular.

Cloud computing. Do you see this as the end of desktop storage?

Questions

1 Describe the benefits and drawbacks to a rural school in moving to a cloud-computing model.
2 What are the implications of cloud computing to computer programmers?

Chapter 10
Hardware

Specification coverage
- The definition of hardware
- Different equipment that constitutes the hardware that makes up a computer system
- Recent developments in hardware

Learning outcomes
- You should be able to describe and explain the fundamental pieces of hardware required to make a functioning computer system.
- You should be able to discuss how developments in different hardware technologies (including memory and processor) are leading to exciting innovative products being created, for example, in the mobile and gaming industries.
- You should be able to categorise devices as input or output depending on their function.

Introduction

In Chapter 9 we looked at the parts that make up a computer system. Hardware is a name given to a collection of physical 'things' that when put together in a certain way form a 'system'.

The human body could be looked on as a collection of hardware. First, you have your brain, not the thought processes that go on inside it, but the physical organ. Then, you have the internal hardware that keeps your body working such as your heart, lungs and digestive system.

You also have 'devices' for taking onboard different information such as the eyes for visual data, your hands that use the sense of touch for tactile information, your ears for sound information and not forgetting your tongue for your sense of taste.

All this information is processed and stored in your brain while you are still alive.

Your body has ways of outputting information too. This involves using speech as well as movements, expressions and gestures that you can make with your face and body.

So, hardware basically refers to parts or components of a system that can be physically touched, although there are not many of us that could truly say that they would like to touch someone's brain – yuck!

Now, let's now take a look at the hardware components of a computer and how they fit together to form a system.

Computer hardware: system unit

Within a computer system there are basically two types of hardware. The hardware within the system consists of the CPU (central processing unit), which is situated on a printed circuit board called the motherboard.

There is the hard disk drive, the RAM (random access memory), optical drive and other circuit boards such as the graphics and sound cards.

These are all regarded as hardware because if you removed the case you could physically touch the devices – although you should *not* do this unless you know what you are doing.

The CPU (central processing unit)

This internal device is often referred to as the 'computer's brain' and it is the piece of hardware that is responsible for the 'compute' in computer. If you did not have the CPU, you would not have a computer.

Just like our brain, the CPU's purpose is to process data. It does this by performing functions such as searching and sorting data and calculating and decision-making using the data.

What this means is that for every task that you carry out on a computer, whether it is designing a spreadsheet, writing an email, playing a game or searching the internet, the CPU will deal with all of the data-processing associated with the task. Without a CPU none of these tasks would be possible.

The history of the CPU is very interesting. At the heart of a CPU is what is called the processor. Its name tells you what it does. The first CPU chip was invented in 1971. It was basically a 4-bit processor designed for a calculator. Its instructions were 8 bits long. Program and data were separate.

Since these early days of CPUs with a single-core processor, there have been many changes to the brain in our computer.

Processor speed has doubled every few years. The first big change to the CPU was the addition of a second processor resulting in what are called dual-core processors. Each processor has its own cache and controller. The benefit of this is that each processor functions as efficiently as a single processor. Because the two processors are linked together, they can perform most operations much faster than a single processor can.

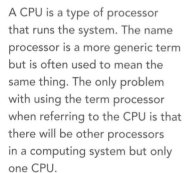

Key term

A CPU is a type of processor that runs the system. The name processor is a more generic term but is often used to mean the same thing. The only problem with using the term processor when referring to the CPU is that there will be other processors in a computing system but only one CPU.

Imagine you have a task of making breakfast of buttered toast and a cup of tea. However fast you work, some things need your full attention. You cannot butter the toast and pour the tea at the same time. But if you had a second person to help, they could make the toast and you could make the tea. The process would then be much faster (providing you were each given the correct instructions, of course).

A photograph of a modern quad-core processor. How many processors would this chip have?

Technology has not stopped with dual-core processors. The next step was quad-core processors, followed by hexa-core processors containing six cores. Some computers even have octa-core processors containing eight cores. You may be thinking that each addition multiplies the processing power of a single-processor machine, but it does not always work like this. The software running on the machine has to be designed to take full advantage of all the processors.

Some processors designed for mobile devices can even interpret Java bytecode directly. Java instructions, or bytecodes, are not like other software programs. The code needs to be adapted to suit the hardware and software it works within. Designers have to use a compiler to adapt the code to individual environments and operating systems. Programs must be offered for many different operating systems. Java bytecode is interpreted by any Java virtual machine or translated into the machine code of the system. The processor acts as a Java virtual machine and executes Javabyte codes. This saves time and processing.

The CPU undertakes the instructions it receives from programs in what is called a cycle. If we go back to the making the toast and tea example: if you worked faster you could produce the breakfast quicker. Perhaps the addition of a quicker kettle would help too. The CPU not only has multiple cores, it has speed. The speed of the CPU is measured in how many cycles it can perform in a second. The name given to one cycle per second is a hertz. A CPU that processes one million cycles per second is said to have a speed of one megahertz (MHz), and a CPU that can handle one billion cycles per second is said to have a clock speed of one gigahertz (GHz).

Having a very high CPU speed is a good thing, because more instructions per second get executed. The problem is that the faster the processor, the hotter it gets, and the more power it needs.

Most people do not notice any speed differences between one processor speed and the next speed higher, that is unless they play the very latest computer games. And if we go back to our breakfast analogy, however fast you work and however many friends you have to help you, if the instructions are not clear and the things you need are not available, you will not be any faster. With CPUs, programmers have a part to play in maximising the speed and cores they have.

Question

Describe the purpose of the CPU.

Motherboard

Motherboards link the CPU to the memory and other hardware.

A photograph of a motherboard. Can you locate the CPU?

The motherboard is like your nerves – the essential connections that send and receive signals throughout your body. The CPU computes data and uses the motherboard to receive and send signals to things like the hard drives (storage). The motherboard is also responsible for holding all of the computer settings such as time and date. As with the CPU, motherboards have speeds as well, called bus speeds.

A bus is the circuit that connects one part of the motherboard to another. The more data the motherboard bus can handle at any one time, the faster the system. The speed of the bus is also measured in megahertz. Motherboards have many buses; each one transfers data from one computer component to another.

Question

Describe the purpose of the computer's motherboard.

Graphics cards

When using programs such as computer games or those that require 3D images, the graphics card is just as important as a good screen. The graphics card supports the CPU. It has a processor like the CPU. However, it is especially designed to control screen images. Imagine having a friend who is very good at drawing. When you need to illustrate something, rather than do it yourself you ask your friend to do it for you. This is how the graphics card works: it helps out the CPU whenever graphics are needed. It does nothing else, but this can be a very hard task.

Remember that the images you see on your screen are made of thousands of tiny dots called pixels. Most screens display well over a million pixels, and the computer has to decide what to do with each and every one in order to create the image that you see on the monitor. It is the job of the graphics card to translate all the ones and zeros into pictures and words.

To make a 3D image, the graphics card has to work even harder than it does for 2D. First, it creates a wire-frame image using straight lines, then it fills in the frame with pixels. The name given to this process is rasterising. Then texture, colour and lighting effects are added. The graphics card has to do all this over 60 times a second during a video game.

The graphics card can be a separate circuit that slots into the computer. The advantage of this type of card is that it can be upgraded. However, the graphics card is an integral part of the motherboard in laptops and handheld devices and cannot be changed.

The graphics card consists of two components:

- A video chip set. The video chip creates the signals that the screen must receive to form an image.
- Random access memory (RAM). Memory is necessary, since the video card must be able to remember a complete screen image at any time.

Questions

1 Why would a gaming computer need a high-specification machine?
2 Why would a gaming computer need a high-specification graphics card?

Memory

Just as we have different kinds of memory, such as memory associated with walking, talking or other motor skills and short- and long-term data memories, there are a number of different types of memory in computer systems.

Memory in a computer system.

If you recall the earlier section on memory allocation you will remember how the computer creates blocks of memory. So using the diagram above let's look at how this works.

The CPU cannot fetch the data it needs directly from the hard disk. This is because even the slowest modern CPU processes data about 50 times faster than the fastest hard disk. So we need fast memory and the fastest memory is cache.

Let's look at what the memory stores. The most important block of memory is the operating system, then all the drivers for the connected devices.

The cache is very high-speed memory and it draws the data from memory called RAM as it is needed. RAM is much faster than the hard disk but even RAM is not fast enough for the CPU. You will see RAM described as 128- or 256-bit rate, but CPUs now often run at over 2 GHz. Computing devices need cache memory. But the problem is not only the speed of the memory device, but also how long it takes to fetch the data.

The cache's memory controllers have to predict what piece of data the CPU will need next. They then collect it from RAM and add it to their high-speed memory. This speeds up the system's performance. It is the operating system that has to control all this. RAM can be supplemented by virtual memory but each step takes time and the hard disk is much slower than the RAM, which in turn is slower than the cache.

The data transfer between operating system and all the input and output devices happens through the virtual nerves in the motherboard using a computer program called a driver.

The driver has to translate electrical signals to and from the devices connected to the system so that the operating system and other programs can control them or receive data from them.

Cache

To understand how cache works, let's start with an example. You have lots of schoolbooks you need each week stored in desk drawers in your bedroom upstairs. For our example, let's say you are downstairs ready for school but you cannot get the books yourself. You have to ask your mother or friend to go upstairs, find them and get them for you. But then imagine how much quicker it would be if your mother or friend knew what books you would need and when you would need them, so kept them close at hand downstairs, passing them to you as soon as you needed them. They then only put them back with all the others in your drawers when they knew you would not need them for some time. This is how cache works. Of course, it cannot store all of your data: it has limited size and so it has a limit to how much it can store.

Cache technology uses very fast but small amounts of memory to speed up slower but larger memory types.

Cache memory is not only used inside your computer. It also helps in systems when data is transferred from very slow data sources, like the internet. Internet connections are the slowest links to your computer, so web browsers use their own cache on the web server to do the same task as your computer's cache, but for web pages. External hard drives also have their own cache memory.

Question

Why is cache as important as clock speed?

Random access memory (RAM)

You know that feeling when you are revising for tests and you feel that your brain is about to explode with too much information? Well, your computer would feel like that if it wasn't for the hard drive. When you are working on your computer you only use a small amount of the information that is stored and because of this the computer transfers from the hard drive to the random access memory (often abbreviated as RAM, or simply called 'memory'). The cache memory is taken from the RAM when needed. If we go back to the schoolbook example, some of your most used books this week are taken from your desk drawer and stored at the top of the stairs.

A photograph of a RAM module.

The advantage of using the RAM for the storage of whatever you are working on is that RAM, while not as quick as cache, is fast. In fact, it is much faster than any disk. What this means for you is that there is far less time waiting and more time being productive.

In the same way that the CPU needs RAM in order to work efficiently, RAM is necessary on the graphics card as it has to keep the entire screen image in its memory. When handling graphics, the CPU sends its data to the video card. The video processor forms a picture of the screen image and stores it in what is called the frame buffer. This picture is a large bitmap.

Some graphics cards use a special memory called VRAM (video RAM). A VRAM cell is made up of two ordinary RAM cells, which are fixed together. This double cell allows the processor to *simultaneously* read and write new data at the same RAM address.

You may now be asking the question: 'If RAM is so fast, why not put everything in it? In fact, why have a hard disk at all?' The answer to that question is because RAM is 'volatile'. What that means is as soon as the computer is shut down, whether intentionally or accidentally, everything in RAM disappears. Just imagine waking up each morning and remembering nothing that you had ever done before, not being able to talk, walk and eat. All of the memory devices we have looked at so far are just like this.

It is not a good idea to rely on RAM to hold everything. A hard disk drive, on the other hand, stores its information whether the power is on or off. Computing devices need somewhere safe to store data when they are switched off. For this they use either hard drives or flash memory.

Hard disk drive

The original Apple iPod music player was not much more than a small hard disk drive. Hard drives are efficient computer memory devices that use magnetism to store data.

The CPU in your computer is the brainy bit that does all the thinking but it's the hard disk drive that lets you store your data, music, photos, music files and text documents. It is also the hard disk drive that holds the programs.

The slowest type of memory is the hard disk drive, but it is the biggest memory device in terms of the amounts of data it can hold. All of the information that is stored within your computer is stored on its hard disk drive. When you switch your device on it is the hard disk that first sends the operating data to the RAM, cache and CPU.

You never see that actual hard disk drive because it's sealed inside a special housing within the case of the computer or device. In a similar way to your long-term memory, the hard disk drive can hold information almost forever – with or without electricity.

Most modern hard disks can have billions of bytes of storage space on them, which means that you can create, save and download files for months or years without fear of using up all the drive's storage space. If you do manage to fill up your hard disk, your operating system will start informing you by way of a message on your screen saying something like: 'You are running low on disk space'. Don't worry: this will happen well in advance of any storage problems occurring.

Read-only memory (ROM)

We found out that RAM forgets what it knows when the power goes off. There is another type of memory called read-only memory (ROM) that doesn't forget when it is switched off.

ROM chips have data pre-installed on them during manufacture. The information is stored on them permanently and cannot ever be changed. This makes them excellent for small mobile devices where they hold the operating system.

Question	

In the world of computing, what is bus width?

Flash memory

Small portable devices like MP3 players, phones and cameras need small portable memory. They use special chips called flash memory to store information permanently. Flash memory has certain things in common with both ROM and RAM as it remembers information when the power is off but it can also be erased and rewritten many times. You also find flash memory in memory sticks.

Flash memory does not use magnetism like hard disk drives; it uses a transistor that stays switched on (or switched off) when the power is turned off. Remember that computers remember everything in binary, so this system works well with all computing needs.

Solid-state hard drives are really large flash memory disks. Because they have no moving parts they are much faster and smaller than traditional hard drives.

Question

What is the brain of the computer called?

Is it better to have more memory or a faster processor?

This is often the biggest question manufacturers and computer buyers have to consider, particularly with regard to RAM. As we have seen in earlier chapters, whenever the computer is manipulating an information string it is placed in the memory to be retrieved or manipulated later. Each block of memory, whether used or not, is allocated by the program.

Once all the usable memory space is filled, the computer has to store temporary data on the hard drive in a space referred to as a swap file. Once in a swap file the CPU has to undertake a two-step process to first write then read the data, rather than a single-step process of reading the data from faster memory.

If we add to this the speed difference between the very fast RAM and the comparatively slow hard drive, you can see how extra memory of the right type of RAM can be just as useful as a faster CPU.

Question

Computer A is a quad-core processor with a clock speed of 2 GHz. Computer B is a single core processor with a clock speed of 2.8 GHz. Explain why the computer with the higher clock speed may not be the faster one.

Optical drives

Optical drives retrieve and/or store data on optical disks such as compact disks (CDs), digital versatile disks (DVDs) and Blu-ray disks (BDs). Burning data to BDs, CDs and DVDs is the most common method of copying and backing up data at home. You have probably done it yourself.

Data is burned on to the surface of an optical disk using a laser contained within the drive. The laser is also used to read the data from the disk.

The typical storage capacity of a CD is 650 MB of data whereas a single-sided DVD can store up to 4.7 GB of data. A double-sided DVD can store 9 GB.

CDs and DVDs use a red laser to read and write data. BDs use a blue–violet laser, hence the name Blu-ray. BDs hold 25–50 GB of data and some new types can store 500 GB on a single disk by using 20 layers.

Basically there are two types of optical media:
- CD-ROM, DVD-R and BD-R, which indicates that the media is read-only memory. This means that data can only be written once and after that occasion the disk cannot be written to again. The disks are writable but not rewritable. They can, however, be read and replayed endless times.
- CD-RW, DVD-RW and BD-RW, which indicates that the media are rewritable This means that data can be repeatedly written to and then erased from the disk.

One problem with optical media is that the different companies that manufacture them have not agreed on a standard format and because of this you will see numerous types of DVD such as DVD-R, DVD+R, DVD-RW and DVD+RW. You should always make sure you buy the correct type of optical media for the device that is within your computer.

Computer hardware: peripherals

We have now considered the hardware that forms the system unit, but as you are probably aware there are many devices that exist outside the computer that are referred to as hardware. Basically, every hardware device that is outside the system unit is referred to as a peripheral. Even though peripheral devices do not form part of the core system unit, they are often, but not always, partially or completely dependent on the host computer.

Understanding input and output devices is essential to a programmer. But almost all modern computing peripherals require both input and output to do anything useful. Even a sheet of paper has input to record ideas and output to display the ideas.

A mouse, in computing terms, is an input device, yet often has a click when the button is pressed (output) and a cursor movement on screen (output).

Input and output are becoming even more blurred with advanced computer interfaces such as mobile devices and gaming consoles. The role of inputs and outputs is to link our human minds and actions with the computer processor.

One of the main issues with input devices is that they often influence the user's ability to input data. Think about the Etch A Sketch toy: it is easier to draw a square than a circle. The choice of device influences the nature of the input.

In Chapter 9 we looked at input and output in terms of the computer system. We learned that traditional peripherals can be categorised into three different groups: *input, output* and *storage*. Input devices provide data into the computer and include:

■ keyboards
■ mice
■ graphics tablets
■ touchscreens
■ image scanners
■ microphones.

Output devices display or present processed data to the user from the computer and include:

■ monitors
■ printers
■ speakers.

Storage peripherals store data in between work sessions on the computer and include devices such as:

■ external hard drives
■ flash drives.

Let's take a closer look at each of these peripheral devices in turn.

Question

Typically, what technology do hard disk drives employ as a storage mechanism?

Input devices

Keyboards

Along with the mouse (see the next section), the keyboard provides a method for you to interact with the computer. The layout of the keys on a keyboard is similar to the design first used with typewriters and you mostly use them for typing text. There are, however, a number of special keys such as *Ctrl (Control), Esc (Escape)* and *Alt (Alternate)* that are used in conjunction with other keys to perform certain functions. There are also a number of other keys at the top of the keyboard which are referred to as the function keys and are labelled F1, F2, F3 and so on. They may perform certain tasks that are dependent on the software that is being used at the time.

A lot of keyboards are also equipped with a numeric keypad, the layout of which resembles an old calculator (remember those?) and tends to be used by people who were used to using that older technology (bank clerks or payroll staff, for example) to type numbers. Really, as you probably know, it doesn't matter whether you use the number keypad or the numbers across the top of the keyboard to type numbers – it's up to you.

Keyboards also have navigation keys that you use to move around text within a document you have on the screen.

Mice

Mice usually have two buttons. The one on the left is called the *primary* button and the one on the right is the *secondary* button. Many mice also have a small wheel between the two mouse buttons.

As you move the mouse, the cursor (the arrow) on the screen should replicate the movement you have just made with the mouse. You use the left button to choose different menu options, click on icons or select hyperlinks on web pages. You can also click and hold down the left button and use it to select text for formatting, deleting, moving or highlighting.

The right button is used to bring up selection menus, such as a format menu in a word-processing program, for example.

Graphics tablets

Sometimes referred to as *digitisers*, graphics tablets are input devices that are mainly used by graphic designers and artists to enable them to hand-draw images and graphics in a similar manner to how you would draw images using a pencil and paper.

Designers may use a tablet to trace an existing, paper-based image so that it can be replicated on the screen. This method of data capture by either tracing or entering the corners of shapes is referred to as *digitising*.

Graphics tablets consist of a flat surface that is used to 'draw' on, which is done using a special pen-like stylus. Usually, the image does not appear on the tablet itself but is reproduced on the monitor screen in front of the designer.

Recent developments within this area now allow designers to draw directly on monitors that are angled to offer a comfortable drawing position. The particular aspect of the image that a designer is wishing to produce such as a line or a shape is directly reproduced under the stylus nib. Some of the more sophisticated pen styluses are pressure sensitive so that if the designer presses harder on the surface, the line they are drawing becomes thicker; if they lessen the pressure the line becomes thinner. These advances in the technology provide an experience to the designer that is as close to drawing using a pen and paper as possible.

Touchscreens

Touchscreens are visual displays that you can interact with using touch. It is possible to use one or multiple finger gestures without having to use an intermediate device such as a mouse or keyboard. Common input devices that use touchscreens include games consoles, smartphones and tablet computers.

There are a number of different technologies that are employed in the manufacture of touchscreens. The main methods include:

- *Resistive touchscreens.* These touchscreens, often used on mobile and hand-held devices, have been around for many years and they were designed to be used with a plastic stylus. The user first taps on the screen to set up accurate sensing by the digitiser. Any touch will work, even a fingernail is accurate enough to use the screen, but pen styluses are usually used.
- *Capacitive touchscreens.* These touchscreens work by sensing skin contact from your finger. They do not work with pressure; they require your body to touch them to register an action. This prevents them from accidentally recording an action in your bag or pocket. If you want to use a handwriting tool on the screen you need a special stylus which has been designed to fool the digitiser into thinking it has been touched by human skin. This type of touchscreen is used in Apple's iPad.

Image scanners

These devices work by optically scanning images, printed text, handwritten documents or even objects and converting it into a digital representation.

The most common type of scanner is a flat-bed scanner, which comprises a top glass pane, under which there is a bright light that illuminates the pane and a moving optical array that contains three rows of sensors with red, green and blue filters.

Microphones

These input peripheral devices convert sound data into an electronic analogue signal, which is converted into digital information by the system unit's sound card. The information can then be manipulated via available software.

Output devices

Monitors

These output peripheral devices provide the main visual display for a computer user. In the past they used cathode-ray tubes (CRTs) just like the massive old televisions your grandparents used to watch. As with televisions, since the 1990s liquid crystal display (LCD) technology has all but taken over.

Initially, LCDs were used in laptops because they needed less power to work and they were light in weight. In the latter half of the 1990s, LCD desktop monitors started to appear and now it is rare to see a CRT monitor in use anywhere.

A variation of LCD technology, TFT-LCD, is now the most dominant technology in use for computer monitors.

The big advantages with TFT-LCD monitors are that they consume less power, they take up less space on a desktop and they are considerably lighter.

The latest development in monitors is the organic light-emitting diode (OLED) display. This offers higher contrast and improved viewing angles compared with LCDs. The disadvantage with OLED is, at present, the cost, but prices will probably drop as the technology becomes more popular.

Printers

Printers are devices that provide a hard copy of documentation by printing text, graphs or illustrations on paper. There are a lot of different types of printers, too many to cover here in detail, so we will briefly look at the most popular.

With regard to the technology that printers use, they fall into the following categories:

- *Ink-jet printers.* These work by spraying small ionised droplets of coloured ink on the paper to produce an image. Magnetised plates direct the coloured ink on to the paper to produce the picture or text you want to print. Ink-jet printers are almost always colour printers and offer a range of different printing resolutions. The best photo printers have more than four ink colours to produce a better quality photographic image. Ink-jet printers are not quite as good as laser printer for general office use but can be much cheaper to buy than laser printers. However, the ink cartridges are quite expensive to use per page printed and ink-jet printers are much slower than laser printers. Colour ink-jet printers can also print in black and white.

- *Dot-matrix printers.* These are a kind of impact printer that creates characters and illustrations by striking pins against an ink ribbon to print closely spaced dots in the appropriate shape. Dot-matrix printers don't produce particularly high-quality documents; the quality is determined by the number of pins, which can vary between 9 and 24, and so they are commonly used for printing invoices, purchase orders, shipping forms, labels, and other multi-part forms. They can run at speeds between 50 and 500 characters per second.

- *Laser printers.* These work using a laser beam to produce an electrically charged image of what you want to print on a drum. The drum is then rolled through a special powder called toner and the electrically charged portions of the drum pick up the toner powder while the non-charged areas do not. After the toner powder on the drum has been transferred to the paper, heat and pressure are used to fix the image. Colour laser printers use the same toner-based powder process, but combine four different toner colour powders.

Speakers

Computer speakers or, as they are sometimes called, multimedia speakers, usually plug into the computer and automatically disable the (usually) lower quality built-in speakers.

Speakers are the peripheral output devices that convert the electrical signal coming from the sound card of the computer into audible sound.

Multimedia speakers usually connect to the 3.5 mm jack plug that is sited somewhere on the computer unit. There are also USB speakers that are powered from the USB socket; however, these tend to give a lower power output.

Question

A smartphone: input or output device?

Make a copy of the table below. For each feature of the phone listed in the table, show whether it is an input method, an output method or both. Tick one box in each row on your copy of the table.

Feature	Input	Output	Both
Touchscreen			
End call button			
Microphone			
Speaker			

Storage devices

External hard disk drives

External hard disk drives (HDDs) are regarded as removable storage peripherals and are typically connected using a USB socket. They have what is commonly known as 'plug and play' functionality, which means that there is no need to install any software in order to use them – you literally plug them in and use them.

External HDDs are usually completely multi-system compatible and feature large to very large storage options coupled with a portable design. They are available in 2.5- and 3.5-inch sizes and their capacities range from 160 GB to 3 TB.

External HDDs are available in two formats:

- as a preassembled integrated unit
- or assembled by combining an external enclosure with a USB or another interface with a separately purchased drive.

Other features that external HDDs can offer include biometric security or multiple interfaces; however, these do come at a higher cost.

Flash drives

Flash drives are data-storage devices that comprise flash memory (a non-volatile computer storage chip that can be electrically erased and reprogrammed) coupled with an integrated USB interface. They are removable and rewritable media and are conveniently small in size.

Some flash drives offer up to 100,000 write/erase cycles, although this does depend on the exact type of memory chip used. It is widely considered that flash drives have taken over the tasks that CD-ROMs used to do a while ago. They are smaller, faster, have thousands of times more capacity, and are more durable and reliable because they are solid state (that is, they have no moving parts).

Smartphones and tablet computers

Smartphones and tablet computers are complete systems but they do connect to computers via networking and USB connections and therefore can be regarded as peripherals. They store data such as music, contacts, documents and so on for the owner to use when they are away from their computer.

A smartphone.

Smartphones and tablet computers are mobile devices that are usually built on a mobile operating system with advanced computing capability and connectivity.

The first smartphones to emerge on to the market combined the functions of a personal digital assistant with a mobile phone. However, later models added a portable music player, GPS navigation and lower-end compact digital and video camera functionality to basically create one mobile multimedia device.

These days, modern smartphones include very high-resolution screens and fast web browsers that can display standard web pages as well as mobile-optimised sites. The data is provided via high-speed connectivity through WiFi and mobile broadband.

Tablet computers, or as they are more commonly known, tablets, are basically mobile computers that are integrated into a thin, flat unit that uses a touchscreen rather than a mouse or a keyboard. In order to type on a tablet, a virtual keyboard can be called up. A physical keyboard also can be connected using Bluetooth or the USB port of the device.

In 2010, Apple released the iPad; this is widely thought of as when tablet computers came of age. It used a similar operating system and touchscreen technology to the company's successful iPhone and it was the first mobile computer tablet to achieve global success. Since then, other manufacturers have produced their own versions using a variety of different operating systems.

Question

What is the name and purpose of the printed circuit board inside a computer?

Chapter 11
CPU (Central Processing Unit)

Specification coverage
■ The purpose of the CPU

Learning outcomes
■ You should be able to describe the purpose of the processor (CPU).
■ Understand how different components link to a processor (ROM, RAM, I/O, storage, and so on).
■ You should be able to explain the effect of common CPU characteristics on the performance of the processor. These should include clock speed, number of cores and cache size/types.

Introduction

In Chapter 8 we looked at what the CPU did in a computer system and how it interacted with other hardware like the motherboard and RAM. But many new computing devices are portable mobile devices. Mobile processors are designed specifically for use in computers where the device is carried from place to place rather than being on a desktop. These new processors are used in everything from laptop computers to mobile phones.

Mobile CPU and processors

Mobile devices are not connected to a power socket all the time, so they need a long battery life. They are also small, so do not have the space for things like fans to keep the CPU cool. This makes them prone to overheating. These design considerations are the reason for the major differences between desktop and mobile CPUs.

So what are the main differences?
■ The first difference is the processor clock speed. The cooling requirements of any portable device require a processor that does not create too much heat. Portable processors always have lower clock speeds than their desktop equivalent as this lowers the amount of heat that they produce.
■ The physical size of the portable device means that there is not much space, so most modern mobile processors also have other components integrated

into the processor itself. These components often include things like wireless networking.

■ Mobile processors are also optimised for very low power consumption.

Most modern smartphones have a dedicated processor for GSM (Global System for Mobile Communications) and another (potentially multi-core) general-purpose processor for the user interface and applications. This processor is known as the application processor (AP), not the CPU as in other computing devices.

Question

What is a clock cycle and why is it important?

The GSM processor is often referred to as the BP processor after its function as a baseband radio processor, meaning that it handles the WiFi and Bluetooth links.

Baseband data is sent as a digital signal through a single channel that uses the full bandwidth of the media. The communication is bidirectional, which means that the same channel is used both to send and to receive signals.

There is an important difference between baseband and broadband, which sends information as an analogue signal that shares the channel with other users. Each transmission is assigned its own portion of the bandwidth. This means that lots of different transmissions are possible at the same time.

Broadband communication is also only one directional, so in order to send and receive, two pathways are needed. This is usually done in a single cable by assigning a frequency for sending and assigning a different frequency for receiving.

If we return now to our BP processor (baseband not broadband), originally each processor had its own memory (RAM and flash), peripherals, clock speed, and so on but the search for smaller, more compact systems has led to a single RAM and flash chip being divided by assigning portions of the RAM and flash to each of the two processors.

Question

Describe briefly the main differences in the processors used in mobile devices compared to desktop computers. Give reasons for the differences mentioned.

Multi-core processors in smartphones and tablets

As we discovered in Chapter 8, a core is simply a distinct processing unit within a CPU. Most desktop and laptop computers have multi-core processors, but what about mobiles?

At first, smartphones had a single core, which was more than sufficient to handle the applications available. But modern smartphones and tablets have CPU-intensive applications and users want to multi-task; for example, many users are watching a video, listening to music and playing a game all at the same time. It is hard to push the 'clock speed' as doing this increases power consumption. As we have seen, this is not what we want as the battery will not last long.

With dual-core processors, one core can process the game, while another processes the music. In this way, none of the cores are pushed to their limit and the overall power consumption of the phone is lower. The drawback is that many mobile programs are still not optimised for using multiple cores.

New developments

In Chapter 8 we looked at the clock speed of processors and explored how having a fast clock speed and multi-core processor was of little value without cache, RAM and the programs to support it. This becomes even more complex when we explore developments in mobile processors.

New designs allow CPUs to run at the same clock rate or at an even lower clock rate than older CPUs used in desktop computers, but to get more instructions completed per clock cycle. This makes it very difficult to use clock rates to compare processors made by different companies.

Smartphones and mobile devices, such as tablet computers, are equipped with more advanced embedded chipsets that can do far more tasks at the same time, providing they have been programmed correctly.

The latest improvements are in the development of an integrated CPU and graphics processing unit (GPU).

Cache

In Chapter 8 we discovered how cache is used to feed data to the CPU. We also learned how the aim of cache was to feed the required data to the CPU as fast as possible so that it is not slowed down due to a lack of data.

You will probably come across references to level 1, 2 and even 3 cache. L1 is short for level 1 cache and this is always built into the CPU. L2 is short for level 2 cache and this originally was external to the CPU on a separate microprocessor chip, but many modern processors now have this built in too. It is also sometimes called the secondary cache.

As more and more CPUs begin to include L2 cache in their architectures, level 3 cache (L3) is the name given to the extra cache that is built into motherboards between the microprocessor and the main memory.

When the CPU finds data in the cache it is called a cache hit. References not found in the cache are called cache misses. When a cache miss occurs, the cache control mechanism must fetch the missing data from the RAM and place it in the cache. The size and organisation of the cache are vitally important.

Cache organisation

There are three key principles involved:

- *Temporal locality*: when the CPU accesses the data and the cache knows that the same data is likely to be needed again, so it stores it ready for when it is needed.
- *Spatial locality*: when the CPU accesses a particular location in memory and the cache knows that it will also need to access data that is stored close to the original data, so it fetches that as well.
- *Sequential locality*: when the CPU accesses data and knows that it is likely that it will need data in the location of $s + 1$ so fetches that as well.

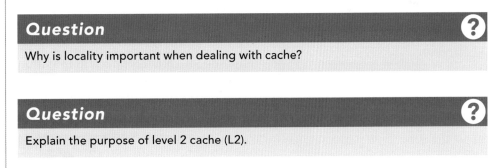

Question

Why is locality important when dealing with cache?

Question

Explain the purpose of level 2 cache (L2).

Cache size

There is no fixed cache size in CPUs, but the faster the CPU, the larger the L2 cache needs to be. The size of the cache refers to the size of the data store. A typical L2 cache is 512 KB, but can be as high as 1 MB or even 2 MB.

Within the CPU itself, L1 cache is usually from 8 to 64 KB.

The more cache the system has, the more likely it is to register a hit when it accesses the RAM and so it will operate faster.

Other types of cache

In Chapter 8 we also explored how cache relates to other aspects of computing. Away from the CPU we have cache for programs, the most common being a web browser cache. Cache here serves the same purpose: it saves time when fetching frequently used data.

Whatever web browser you use to surf the web, it will have a folder in which certain items that have been downloaded are stored for future access. Your browser assumes that you will want to view these again and so holds them in cache. Of course, it is not as sophisticated as the cache in a CPU and it only performs temporal locality as an organisation method.

Web cache stores graphic images, photographs and even entire web pages. When you visit a page on a website, your computer first checks its cache folder to see if it already has those images and, if so, it won't take the time to download them again.

This makes page loading much faster, but can be a problem for web designers when they change items on a page and test the changes to only see the original page being drawn from the cache.

Another problem is that cache folders can get very big and can occupy a large amount of hard disk drive space. It is advisable to empty the cache regularly and to limit the cache size.

Cache in programming

Once you understand the concepts of cache both to the CPU and to the way that computing systems work, you can use these concepts in your own programming for various applications and purposes.

In programming, a cache library can be used for storing database queries for later use. It can also be used to store rendered pages to save generating them again.

Chapter 12
Memory

Specification coverage
- Volatile and non-volatile memory
- Virtual memory

Learning outcomes
- You should know the differences between non-volatile and volatile memory.
- Understand the purpose of both types of memory and when each should be used.
- You should be able to explain the purpose of virtual memory and cache memory.
- You should be able to explain the concept that data and instructions are stored in memory and processed by the CPU.

Introduction

We have already explored some types of memory. In Chapter 11 we looked at cache, for example. The word 'memory' is used to refer to the internal storage areas within a computer system and is often associated with the memory chips that form part of the electronics of a computer. The word 'storage' is often associated with what is referred to as 'secondary storage', which will be covered in Chapter 13.

The main CPU and related memory components inside a computer are based on what are called semiconductors, sometimes referred to as computer chips. Actually a computer chip is an electronic circuit embedded on to a semiconducting material. A semiconductor is something that will conduct electricity under some conditions but not others. It is not hard to see how such a material could be used in a device that needs only to remember ones and zeros.

There are two main categories of chip-based memory: volatile and non-volatile.

Volatile memory

Volatile memory is computer memory that requires a power supply in order to maintain stored data. In other words, volatile memory will store information as long as power is being supplied to it. However, the moment that the power is turned off, the information is lost. Volatile memory is often referred to as 'temporary memory'.

The RAM (random access memory) in your computer is a type of volatile memory. If there was a power cut when you were using your computer, any data that was stored on it when the power was disconnected is immediately erased. This is the reason why you should get into the habit of frequently saving your work to the hard disk (non-volatile memory – see below) when you work on your computer.

Normal RAM is *dynamic* (called DRAM). The advantage of the DRAM is that each stored data bit takes up a very small space. The disadvantage is that to achieve this the stored charge does not last very long, so it has to be refreshed periodically by a control circuit in the RAM stick. Static RAM has six transistors used to store each bit, rather than the single one on DRAM.

Key point

Volatile memory cannot store data when the computing device is turned off. Non-volatile memory can.

Question ?

Explain why some data is stored in RAM when you are running a program.

Question ?

What kind of computer memory is both static and non-volatile?

Several types of DRAM

There are several types of DRAM for computing devices and they are all quite different. This means that they cannot be used on the same motherboard as they are not compatible.

Even when you find compatible DRAM for the same motherboard there will be different types, some more expensive than others. You may see the word latency. Latency is the time it takes for the DRAM to respond. Imagine you are playing your favourite computer game and you are called for dinner. There will be a delay between your being called and your arrival to eat. This is latency.

In DRAM, latency is measured by the number of clicks of the system clock it takes for the DRAM to respond.

As volatile memory is solid state (that is, it has no moving parts), it is able to process data far quicker than non-volatile memory such as hard disks. This is the reason why it is used for the DRAM within computers. We are talking about a latency of a single clock click of around 200 MHz. The latency of the DRAM needs to match the motherboard and CPU.

As we learned in earlier chapters, RAM is where the programs that you wish to use are loaded to from the hard disk. If you were to work with programs directly off the hard disk, the latency would be much longer, and you would find the programs were sluggish and very slow to respond to your requests.

Question

What is the difference between DRAM and RAM?

Buffered DRAM

Most motherboards will hold four sticks of DRAM. But very high-performance computers need more. To enable the motherboards to take more DRAM, special DRAM is needed. The DRAM sticks have what are called buffering chips added. **Buffering** is quite important in computing; in the case of DRAM the buffer controls the amount of electrical current which goes to and from the memory chips at any given time. This makes the DRAM more stable, but it also increases the cost of the DRAM stick and slows the RAM's speed.

Task

Explore the term 'print buffer'.

Question

What type of memory is a memory stick and how does it work?

Non-volatile memory

Non-volatile memory is computer memory that will retain its information whether the power being supplied to it is turned on or switched off. Examples of non-volatile memory include ROM (read-only memory), flash memory, and most types of magnetic computer hard disks and optical disks (see Chapter 10). Interestingly, early computer storage methods such as paper tape and punched cards are also referred to as non-volatile memory.

The purpose of non-volatile memory is to be used as secondary or long-term persistent storage. Secondary storage will be covered in Chapter 13.

Key term

A buffer is a temporary storage area, usually but not always in RAM. The main purpose of a buffer is to act as a holding area, enabling the computer to manipulate data before transferring it to a device.

Virtual memory

The evolution of intelligent memory management procedures within computers has allowed an increase in the use of virtual memory. This is achieved by putting some sections of RAM on the hard disk. Of course, latency times are extended but the RAM capacity is extended as well. The name for this type of RAM is virtual memory.

Why add virtual memory?

Let's say that your computer only has 1 GB of RAM and you attempt to run a few programs that command a memory of around 1.5 GB. Without virtual memory, an error message would appear saying that your memory was full. But with virtual memory, the operating system assigns a part of the hard disk as a part of the RAM memory and keeps the data there.

In our example let's assume that the virtual memory is also 1 GB. The 1 GB actual memory + 1 GB virtual memory = 2 GB of memory. So even though your RAM stick is relatively small in size you can still use memory-intensive applications.

As with everything, unfortunately there is a disadvantage to using virtual memory. Reading data from a hard disk is much slower than reading from solid-state RAM and so the more information that is stored in your hard disk, the slower your system becomes.

Chapter 13
Secondary storage

Specification coverage

- Secondary storage including magnetic, optical and solid-state drives

Learning outcomes

- Understand what secondary storage is and be able to explain why it is required.
- You should be able to describe the most common types of secondary storage.
- Understand how optical media, magnetic media and solid state work.

Introduction

Secondary storage (often also called auxiliary storage), is anything that stores data other than the temporary storage in things like RAM. In a personal computer, secondary storage usually consists of a hard disk and removable media.

External storage is also secondary storage. External secondary storage devices are used to:

- back up data
- add more storage space for files, photographs, videos and so on
- transfer files between computers
- easily transport files without taking your computing device with you
- share files over a network.

Different types of non-volatile secondary storage include the following:

- magnetic storage
- optical storage:
    - compact disk (CD)
    - digital versatile disk (DVD)
    - Blu-ray disk (BD)
- solid-state disk
- USB drive (memory stick or pen drive)
- flash memory card.

Magnetic storage

A magnetic hard disk drive uses moving read and write heads that contain electromagnets. These create a magnetic charge on the disk's surface which contains iron particles that can be given a magnetic charge in one of two directions. Each magnetic particle's direction represents 0 (off) or 1 (on). As you will remember these represent a bit of data that the CPU can recognise.

Advantages

- Very large data storage capacity.
- Stores and retrieves data much faster than an optical disk.
- Data is not lost when you switch off the computer as it is with RAM.
- Cheap per MB compared to other storage media.
- Can easily be replaced and upgraded.

Disadvantages

- Hard disks have moving parts and will eventually fail.
- Crashes can damage the surface of the disk, leading to loss of data.
- Easily damaged if dropped.
- Uses a large amount of power compared to other media.
- Can be noisy.

Optical storage

An optical drive uses reflected light to read data. The optical disk's surface is covered with tiny dents (pits) and flat spots (lands) which cause light to be reflected off them differently. When an optical drive shines light into a pit, the light is not reflected back. This represents a bit value of 0 (off). When the light shines on a flat surface (land) it reflects light back to the sensor, representing a bit value of 1 (on).

Advantages

- Easy to store and carry.
- Optical disks are read in a number of devices such as audio and television systems.
- Very easy to use.
- Long-lasting if looked after properly.

Disadvantages

- Data on write-once disks (CD-R, DVD-R and BD-R) is permanent and cannot be changed.
- Optical disks require special drives to read and write.
- Optical storage is expensive per GB/TB in comparison to other methods.
- There are no standards for longevity tests.
- Can easily be scratched and damaged by heat and light.
- Easily broken.

Solid-state disk

Solid-state disks record data using special transistors that retain their state even when there is no power to them. Because there is no moving actuator arm like on a hard disk drive, they are faster in reading and, in some cases, writing data. They are also more rugged so are not as easily damaged when dropped.

Advantages

- Read speeds are faster than normal hard drives.
- Solid-state hard drives have non-volatile memory, which means that data is stable.
- They are lightweight.
- They are very durable.
- They are free from mechanical problems.
- They require less power than magnetic drives.
- They are silent in use.

Disadvantages

- They have limited storage capacity when compared to normal magnetic hard drives.
- Random write speeds of solid-state drives can be four times slower than normal magnetic hard drives.
- The cost per GB stored is higher than magnetic drives.
- Information can only be erased and written about 100,000 times.

Memory stick (pen drive)

USB flash drives use the same technology as solid-state drives. They are a more compact shape and operate faster than an external magnetic drive due to their lack of moving parts. Flash drives are widely used to transport files and back up data from computer to computer.

Advantages

- The biggest advantage of flash memory sticks is that they are small and easily portable.
- Memory sticks have non-volatile memory, which means that data is stable.
- They do not need internal power.
- They are lightweight.
- They are very durable.
- Adding or deleting files in flash memory is quick and tidy.
- They are free from mechanical problems.
- They require less power than magnetic drives.
- They are silent in use.

Question

Discuss the advantages and disadvantages of using a memory stick and cloud-based storage.

Disadvantages

- The cost per GB stored is higher than magnetic drives.
- Information can only be erased and written about 100,000 times.
- They can break easily.
- They can be lost, misplaced or broken.
- They can be affected by electronic corruption and this can make entire data totally unreadable.

Flash memory card

A memory card or flash memory card is also a solid-state drive using flash memory. These cards are often used with digital cameras, handheld computers, mobile telephones, music players, video-game consoles and other types of small electronic devices.

Advantages

- They are small and easily portable.
- Memory cards have non-volatile memory, which means that data is stable.
- They do not need internal power.
- They are lightweight.
- They are very durable.
- Adding or deleting files in flash memory is quick and tidy.
- They are free from mechanical problems.
- They require less power than magnetic drives.
- They are silent in use.

Disadvantages

- There are many different formats and sizes, making them often only suited to one device and hard to read across devices.
- The cost per GB stored is higher than magnetic drives.
- Information can only be erased and written about 100,000 times.
- They can be lost, misplaced or broken.
- They can be affected by electronic corruption and this can make entire data totally unreadable.

Question

Describe the benefits and drawbacks of a using traditional magnetic hard drive in a laptop computer when compared to a solid-state hard drive.

Chapter 14
Algorithms

Specification coverage
- Understanding algorithms

Learning outcomes
- Understand that algorithms are computational solutions that always finish and return an answer.
- You should be able to interpret simple algorithms to deduce their function.
- You should be able to create algorithms to solve simple problems.
- You should be able to detect and correct errors in simple algorithms.

Introduction

To get a computer to do something, we have to tell it what to do. We do this by using a program. But there are lots of ways of doing the same thing.

To get to school you can walk, go by bus, go on a bicycle or get driven in a car. Each would have its own instructions and to get there you would follow the steps in the instruction. These instructions are called algorithms. These four algorithms accomplish exactly the same goal: you arrive at school. But each algorithm gets you there in a completely different way.

Each algorithm also has a different cost and different speed, and requires different external hardware.

So what is the difference between an algorithm and any other program? Basically an algorithm has a defined outcome, a defined end. In computing, an algorithm is a well-defined procedure that takes a value, or set of values, as input and produces an output.

Without algorithms we would have no spam filters, no sort facilities in things like email software, and we would not be able to search the web.

Algorithms in maths

Before we explore algorithms in code, we need to understand how they work in mathematics. When the word algorithm is used in maths, it refers to a set of steps used to solve a mathematical problem. For example, if you are carrying out a long division for 53 divided by 3 you would have the following algorithm:

How many times does 3 go into 5?
The answer is 1
How many are left over? 2
As 3 will not go into 2 add a 0 (10s).
How many times does 3 go into 20?
The answer is 6 with a remainder of two.

And, of course, the answer is 1.6 with a remainder of 2. If we also insert a 0, it then becomes 20 and we get 1.66 with a remainder of 2. The step-by-step process used to do the long division is called a long division algorithm. Algorithms are used a lot in maths, especially in algebra.

Task

Write a simple algorithm for a set of traffic lights at a busy two-way junction. Cars should be able to go straight on, turn left or right, and pedestrians should be able to cross the roads safely.

Key point

Algorithms are often written in words before being turned into code. You should write each step before attempting to create the program on the computer.

Algorithms in programming

You are creating an algorithm every time you write a program. You are creating a set of steps to perform a task. Your knowledge of mathematical algorithms is essential, as many computing algorithms follow the same processes.

If we examine a piece of code we can convert it from the code to a set of step-by-step instructions. The name for this is reverse engineering.

```
<html>
<head>
<title>PHP Test Page</title>
</head>
<body>
<center><b>
<?php
print "I like computer science";
print "<br>";
print "Steve said \"I like computer science too\""
?>
</b></center>
</body>
</html>
```

The instructions are:

■ Put 'PHP Test Page' on the screen as a heading in the centre of the screen.

■ Next switch to a PHP instruction.

■ Under the heading put: 'I like computer science'.

■ Under this put: 'Steve said I like computer science too'.

Serial and parallel algorithms

Algorithms may also be divided into two groups:

■ serial algorithms, where each step or operation is carried out in a linear order

■ parallel algorithms, where a number of operations are run parallel to each other. Parallel algorithms are used with computers running parallel processors.

Question

Explain the terms serial and parallel.

Algorithms in file compression

All compression uses algorithms. All compression algorithms are classified in computing terms as either *lossless* or *lossy*:

■ Lossless algorithms do not change the content of a file. As the name suggests, there is no loss of file detail, every bit is retained. If you compress a file and then decompress it, nothing has changed. Lossless algorithms are used to compress text and program files.

■ Lossy algorithms achieve better compression by selectively deleting some of the information in the file. These algorithms are used for large images or sound files but not for text or program data. The JPEG and MP3 compression algorithms are lossy.

Question

State two file extensions for an image file.

Algorithms in security

If you program anything that works over the internet and needs to handle confidential information you will have to use what are called 'cryptographic algorithms' to keep the system secure.

Cryptographic algorithms are sequences of rules that are used to encrypt and decipher code. They are algorithms that protect data by making sure that unauthorised people cannot access it.

Most security algorithms involve the use of encryption, which allows two parties to communicate but uses coded messages so that third parties such as hackers cannot understand the communications. Encryption algorithms are used to transform plain text into something unreadable. The encrypted data is then decrypted to restore it, making it understandable to the intended party.

There are hundreds of different types of cryptographic algorithms, but most fit into two classifications: they are either symmetric or asymmetric.

Asymmetric algorithms use two keys: a public key and a private key. The public key can be shared, but, to protect the data, the private key is only stored by the user. Encryption and decryption of data need both private and public keys. For example, data encrypted by the private key must be decrypted by the public key.

Symmetric algorithms are faster than asymmetric algorithms as one key is required. The disadvantage of this system is that both parties know the secret key.

Keeping data secure

When using internet banking a bank card reader provides additional security.

Increasingly, banks are using card readers to add another level of security to their customers' accounts. A bank card reader is a very small, handheld piece of equipment that looks like a pocket calculator. It has a slot into which you place your bank's debit card, and number and function keys.

This is called two-factor authentication. The two factors here are 'something you know', which is the password, and 'something you have', which is the debit card.

When you undertake a transaction online, the bank sends you an eight-digit number. You put your card into the reader, enter your PIN and then type in the bank-generated number. The system uses an asymmetric encryption to generate an eight-digit key that you must use to reply to the bank.

Task

Research the terms asymmetric and symmetric.

Question

Discuss the benefits and drawbacks of a bank using a symmetric key rather than an asymmetric key for its customers to access their accounts.

Chapter 15
Data representation

Specification coverage
- Binary data

Learning outcomes
- Understand that computers use the binary alphabet to represent all data and instructions.
- Understand the terms bit, nibble, byte, kilobyte, megabyte, gigabyte and terabyte.
- Understand that a binary code could represent different types of data such as text, image, sound, integer, date and real number.
- Understand how binary can be used to represent positive whole numbers (up to 255).
- Understand how sound and bitmap images can be represented in binary.
- Understand how characters are represented in binary and be familiar with ASCII and its limitations.
- Understand why hexadecimal number representation is often used and know how to convert between binary, denary and hexadecimal.

Introduction

Computing systems can only store a limited amount of information, even if the limit is very large. To be able to fully understand data representation you need to first understand the differences between digital and analogue data.

Analogue data is continuous, analogous to the actual information it represents. For example, a mercury thermometer is an analogue device. The mercury rises in direct proportion to the temperature. Computers cannot work with analogue information.

Digital data breaks the information up into separate steps. This is done by breaking the analogue information into pieces and representing those pieces using binary digits.

If you think back to the start of the book, you will know that all data on computers is represented in binary data as a sequence of zeros and ones. In Chapter 1 we looked at how to represent numbers using binary and hexadecimal. But it is not just numbers that have to be represented this way.

All text, executable files, images, audio and video have to be denoted in digital data.

Task

Produce a table containing eight rows and two columns. In the left-hand column list eight electrical devices that use analogue data, in the right-hand column list eight electrical items that use digital data.

Question

Explain why computers must use digital not analogue data.

Bits, nibbles and bytes

- *Bit.* We know that a bit has a value of 1 or 0.
- *Nibble.* A nibble is four bits.
- *Byte.* A byte is eight bits.

Bits are so small that we cannot use them for comparison from now on, so we use bytes instead.

Key point

The magic number to remember is 1024.

- *Kilobyte (KB).* A kilobyte is 1024 bytes.
- *Megabyte (MB).* A megabyte is 1,048,576 bytes or it is easier to remember as 1024 kilobytes.
- *Gigabyte (GB).* A gigabyte is 1024 megabytes or 1,048,576 kilobytes.
- *Terabyte (TB).* A terabyte is 1024 gigabytes or 1,048,576 megabytes.
- *Petabyte (PB).* A petabyte is 1024 terabytes or 1,048,576 gigabytes.
- *Exabyte (EB).* An exabyte 1024 petabytes or 1,048,576 terabytes.
- *Zettabyte (ZB).* A zettabyte is 1024 exabytes or 1,048,576 petabytes.
- *Yottabyte (YB).* A yottabyte is 1024 zettabytes or 1,048,576 exabytes.

Question

What is the mathematical difference between a megabyte and a terabyte?

Just to give you an example of what these numbers all mean, if we stored photos of 3 MB in size on a hard drive with these memory volumes this would be the outcome:

Hard drive capacity	Number of 3 MB digital images that could be stored
1 kilobyte (KB)	None
1 megabyte (MB)	None
1 gigabyte (GB)	341
1 terabyte (TB)	349,525
1 petabyte (PB)	357,913,941
1 exabyte (EB)	366,503,875,925
1 zettabyte (ZB)	375,299,968,947,541
1 yottabyte (YB)	384,307,168,202,282,000

Representing text using ASCII

We can encode text using the ASCII standard that associates a seven-bit binary number with each of 128 different characters.

	000	001	010	011	100	101	110	111
0000	NULL	DLE		0	@	P	`	p
0001	SOH	DC1	!	1	A	Q	a	q
0010	STX	DC2	"	2	B	R	b	r
0011	ETX	DC3	#	3	C	S	c	s
0100	EDT	DC4	$	4	D	T	d	t
0101	ENQ	NAK	%	5	E	U	e	u
0110	ACK	SYN	&	6	F	V	f	v
0111	BEL	ETB	'	7	G	W	g	w
1000	BS	CAN	(	8	H	X	h	x
1001	HT	EM	)	9	I	Y	i	y
1010	LF	SUB	*	:	J	Z	j	z
1011	VT	ESC	+	;	K	[	k	{
1100	FF	FS	,	<	L	\	l		
1101	CR	GS	-	=	M	]	m	}
1110	SO	RS	.	>	N	^	n	~
1111	SI	US	/	?	O	_	o	DEL

ASCII stands for American Standard Code for Information Interchange. As we have seen, computers can only understand numbers, so an ASCII code is the numerical representation of characters such from a to z, @ or even an action of some sort.

Question

Discuss the problems with using ASCII for a programmer based in France and producing programs for the local market.

Representing sound data files

The MP3 file format was designed to encode a raw audio file as a sequence of zeros and ones. Let's explore how sound works in more detail.

Sound can only exist where there is some type of medium that can transmit waves. Air and water will transmit sound waves but sound cannot exist in a vacuum (such as in outer space).

If you shout, a sound wave goes from your mouth in all directions. This wave causes changes in the pressure in the air that then hits someone else's eardrums. The brain interprets the movement on the eardrum as sound.

You will have seen how sound waves can be represented in graphical form as in the drawing below.

A sound wave is analogue data. Can you think of a disadvantage of digitising music?

On a computer we store sound in digital format. But to save space we use only a sample of the sound.

Let's look at a simplified version of the sound graph above. An analogue sound wave is divided up into a set of digital signals represented by the bars drawn on the graph below. This can then be stored as zeros and ones as we only have to record the height of the bars.

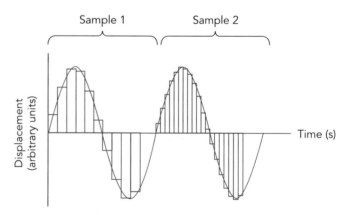

Digitising an analogue sound wave.

In the graph you can see that there are more bars in the second sample. The number of samples per second in an audio file is called the sampling rate and is usually about 44,100 samples per second. We normally write this is 44.1 kilohertz (kHz). If you stored the sound at a higher sampling rate, as shown in sample 2, you would have more data points per second, and better sound, but at a cost in terms of file size.

There is no point in storing sound at a better quality than our hearing system can make use of.

In an MP3 file the sound is compressed so your music becomes almost a twelfth the size of an uncompressed version.

How does MP3 work?

The sound is first split into 12 frequency bands ranging from the high notes (high frequencies) to the low notes (low frequencies). Once the data for all the frequency bands has been recorded, a computer program eliminates the quietest and non-recognisable ones, and this reduces the file size. The science behind this is called psychoacoustics, the study of how the human brain perceives sound. You do not hear the difference as your ears cannot pick up these sounds. Finally, all frequency bands are merged together and written to a single, much smaller file. This process is called compression.

Representing video in data files

A moving image is a sequence of still images called frames which when shown with very short time intervals between each frame fools the brain into believing it is seeing a moving image. The brain smoothes over the change from one image to the next.

With a minimum frame rate of around 20 frames per second needed to stop the moving image flickering, this takes a large number of images and a large amount of data to be stored in memory. We looked at individual images and how they were stored in an earlier chapter.

Computers handle two types of moving image:
- animations
- videos (also called films, movies and video clips).

The main difference between a video and an animation is that with a video, images are captured using a camera.

Representing animation in data files

Animations are drawn not photographic images. They are often drawn with the help of a computer. The difference in programming terms is becoming blurred because videos are often heavily altered using computer techniques and animations used in computer games often look as lifelike as video images.

Data compression

If we do the maths, let's say a full-colour image of 50 mm × 30 mm needs the 3 megabytes (MB) that our earlier images were.

With 20 frames per second, a 5-minute video clip would need 300 seconds of images (5 minutes multiplied by 60 seconds per minute to get the total number of seconds).

To calculate the number of images needed, we need to multiply the number of seconds (300) by the number of images per second (20) giving us a total of 6000 images. Now we need to multiply the number of images by the size of each image (3 MB). We would therefore require 18,000 MB of storage space, almost two gigabytes of memory for a 5-minute video. This is a large amount of memory and if it is to be transferred via the internet we have a major issue. Even processing it in the computer's memory would need a very high-specification machine. We must use compression to make the film usable. For moving images, one common compression technique is called MPEG (Moving Picture Experts Group).

MPEG is similar to JPEG for each of the frames in the sequence, but it performs further compression from one frame to the next by only recording the differences between the frames. If in a scene someone has moved a leg slightly against an unchanging background it only records the change not the background. It simply records that the background has not changed.

Question

State five reasons why software compression is important.

Data standards

To help programmers each data system is controlled by a set of data standards.

Type of data	Standards include
Images	JPEG, GIF, TIFF, BMP, GIF, and so on
Sound	WAV, MP3, AU, and so on
Moving images	QuickTime, MPEG-2, MPEG-4, and so on
Alphanumeric	ASCII, Unicode
Outline graphics/fonts	TrueType, PDF, PostScript, and so on

Key point

All data are numbers, and all numbers are data.

Task

Create your own table of software extensions that involve some sort of compression.

Question

Why are data standards important?

Chapter 16
Software development life cycle

Specification coverage

- Describe the software development life cycle
- The importance of the different stages of the software development life cycle
- Why certain steps happen at different stages of the software development life cycle
- The range of software development life cycle models
- Benefits and issues with the different software development life cycle models

Learning outcomes

- Understand the software development life cycle.
- You should be able to explain what commonly occurs at each stage of the software development life cycle.
- You should be able to identify at which stage of the software development life cycle a given step would occur.
- Understand that there are several life cycle models that can be used (for example, cyclical, waterfall, spiral).
- You should be able to discuss the advantages and disadvantages of these life cycle models.

Definition of the software development life cycle

You probably understand what a life cycle is from science. It is all the stages from start to finish listed as a sequence of stages or steps. The software development life cycle is a structured procedure used for developing software products. It describes the steps called phases of the software cycle and the order in which those phases are carried out. You may hear it referred to by other names such as software life cycle and software process and it is often looked on as an important part of larger systems' development life cycles.

There are a number of models that offer different approaches to the variety of phases that occur during the whole cycle and some software development organisations adopt their own but all have very similar patterns. The basic model is shown on the next page.

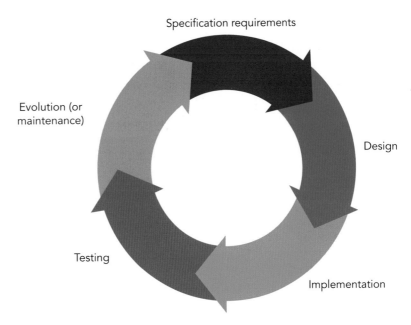

Software development life cycle.

Each stage produces a completed step that is required by the following step in the life cycle:

- A list of what is needed, called 'specification requirements', is provided to allow the design stage to start.
- Code is written during the implementation phase.
- Testing checks that the code written in the implementation phase meets the requirements in the specification.

Stages of the software development life cycle: a general model

Requirements

At this stage, the requirements for the design specification are gathered. This phase is the most important for all the people who have an interest in the project. This is when meetings often take place between the designers, programmers and users. The following questions are asked:

- Who is going to use the software?
- How will they use the software?
- What data should be input into the software?
- What data should be output by the system?

These general questions must get answered during what is called a requirements gathering phase if the project is going to achieve a successful final outcome. This stage then produces a specification of functionality that the software should provide, such as:

- The functions the software should perform.
- The business logic that processes data.
- What data is stored and used by the software.
- How the user interface should work.

This is possibly the most important stage of the design process and yet one of the least understood. It is important that before you produce a 'solution' there is a true understanding of the actual user needs.

The specification is a document listing what the needs of the task are in detail. The designer should constantly refer back to this document to ensure designs are appropriate. You may find that drawing up such a specification will help you to decide how best to answer your assignment.

The deliverable at this stage describes the software as a whole and how it performs, not how it is actually going to do it. There are often key pieces of information in the task itself, so make sure that you list all the requirements defined in your task before you start to design a solution.

Design

It is at this stage that the design of the software begins from the deliverables of the requirements phase. Software architects have ultimate responsibility for the project at this stage, as it is the phase where their focus is greatest. This is where the details on how the software will work are created.

In your project, you will need to plan out how your solution will work. You normally do this using a flowchart. This is done before you start to code anything. You may also want to design the look and feel of the software interface.

Implementation

From the deliverables that come out of the design phase, code is written during the implementation stage, which is usually the longest phase of the software development life cycle. For a developer, this phase is the main focus of the life cycle because this is where the code is produced.

There is the possibility that the implementation stage may overlap with both the design and testing phases.

From your designs you will start to write the code, testing and improving it as you go.

Testing

During the testing phase, the implementation is tested against the specification requirements to ensure that the product is actually providing a solution to the needs addressed and gathered during the requirements phase.

Certain tests such as unit tests and software acceptance tests are carried out during this phase. Unit tests focus on a specific component of the software, while software tests act on the program as a whole.

Evolution (or maintenance)

Even the best software products undergo changes or upgrades once they are delivered to the customer. There can be a number of different reasons for these changes happening, such as a consequence of some unexpected input values into the software. In addition, there may have been some changes in the overall system, which directly affect the software operations. It is very important that the software be developed to allow changes that could happen during the post-implementation period.

Life cycle models

Waterfall model

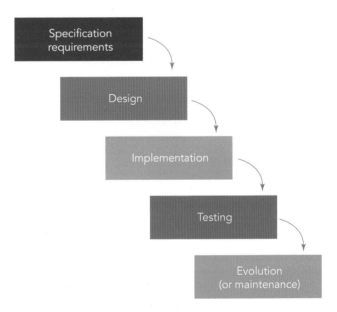

The waterfall model. Why do you think it is called that?

This is by far the most common of life cycle models. It is also sometimes referred to as a linear-sequential life cycle model. Its popularity is probably due to its being very simple to understand and use. In a waterfall software development model, each phase must be totally completed prior to the next phase beginning. At the end of each of the phases, reviews are carried out to determine if the project is proceeding correctly and a decision is made as to whether the project should be continued or discarded. The difference between this model and the previously mentioned general model is that in the waterfall model phases do not overlap.

Advantages

- Simple and easy to use.
- Easy to manage due to the rigidity of the model – each phase has specific deliverables and a review process.
- Phases are processed and completed one at a time.
- Works well for smaller projects where requirements are very well understood.

Disadvantages

- Cannot be used where the software requirements are likely to change.
- There are lots of risks and uncertainty in this model.
- No working software is produced until very late in the life cycle.
- Not a good model for complex projects.
- Not a very good system model for long and ongoing projects.
- There is no real flexibility in this model.

Incremental model

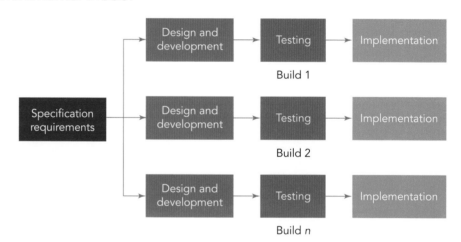

The incremental model.

The incremental model is similar to the waterfall model. Within this model, more than one development cycle occurs at the same time, making this life cycle a kind of 'multi-waterfall' cycle.

Cycles are divided into smaller, more easily managed iterations and each iteration passes through the specification requirements, design and development, testing, and implementation phases.

A working version of software is produced during the first build, resulting in working software being available early on during the software life cycle.

Advantages

■ Produces working software quickly and early on in the software development life cycle.

■ A more flexible model meaning that it is less expensive to change scope and system requirements.

■ Each iteration is an easily managed stage.

■ Easier to manage risk because problems are identified and handled during iteration, not at the end.

■ Easier to test and debug the software early in the build process.

Disadvantages

■ Each phase of an iteration is fixed with no real parallel development.

■ Problems can arise with software architecture, as not all of the requirements are worked out before the start of the software life cycle.

Task

Imagine that you are a company developing a new computer game. Write a software development plan using the incremental model.

Question

Why would a software development company choose the incremental development model rather than the waterfall model for a large project involving several programmers?

Spiral model

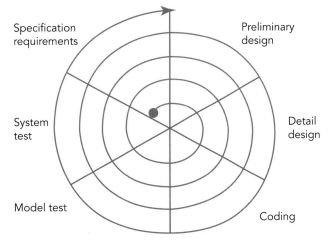

The spiral model.

The spiral model places emphasis on risk analysis and usually has four spirals (repeat turns through the six phases):

- planning
- risk analysis
- engineering
- evaluation.

The software development spirals through six design phases from the start point, repeatedly passing through the various phases. You will notice that the start point is the specification requirements phase, it is where the specification requirements are gathered and the risk is assessed. The spiral continues phase by phase then repeats the cycle, each turn building on the baseline spiral, and revisits the design phases.

During the preliminary design phase, the design requirements are gathered and this is then followed by risk analysis in the detail design phase where a process is undertaken to identify risk and create alternative solutions. A prototype is then produced.

The actual software is produced within the coding phase, which is then tested. During the system test phase, customers can evaluate the output of the project before the project continues to visit all the stages again during the next spiral. In the spiral model, each completed section represents progress, and the radius of the spiral represents the cost of the project. The more iterations of the processes, the more costly the project.

Advantages

- Excellent model for very large projects.
- High degree of risk analysis and development.
- Software is produced and tested early within the software life cycle.

Disadvantages

- A very expensive choice for smaller projects.
- Can be a costly model to adopt as the process never really ends.
- Risk analysis requires highly specific expertise.

V-shaped model

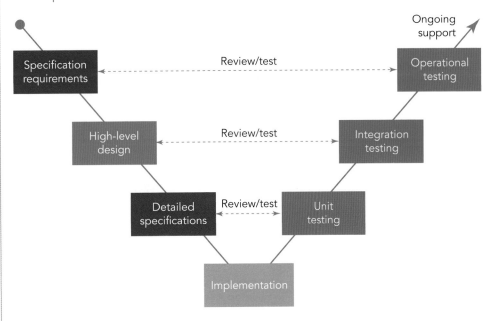

The V-shaped model.

Similar to the waterfall model, the V-shaped life cycle follows a sequence where each phase is completed before the next phase starts. A difference between this model and the waterfall model is that the testing phase is regarded as being much more important.

Specification requirements start the life cycle model in the same way as they did in the waterfall model; however, before the development phase commences, a system test plan is produced. The test plan concentrates on testing the software against the functionality specified.

The high-level design stage concentrates on software architecture. An integration test plan is also produced in this stage with the purpose of testing the ability of the separate pieces of software to work together. The low-level design stage is where the actual program components are designed as well as the unit tests being carried out.

As in the waterfall model, the implementation phase is where all programming occurs.

Advantages

- A good choice for small projects that have easy-to-understand requirements.
- Each stage delivers specific aspects of the project.
- Greater possibility of success over the waterfall model as a consequence of the development of test plans early on during the life cycle.
- Simple and easy to use.

Disadvantages

- As the software is produced during the implementation phase, there are no early prototypes of the software.
- Very little flexibility.
- Very structured in a similar way to the waterfall model.

Task

Develop a software development plan for one of your own programs.

Question

Discuss the benefits and drawbacks of the spiral model compared to the waterfall model in software development.

Chapter 17
Prototyping

Specification coverage

- Knowledge of prototyping and its purpose
- Benefits and issues with prototyping
- Use of prototyping

Learning outcomes

- Understand what prototyping is.
- You should be able to discuss the advantages and disadvantages of using prototyping when developing solutions.
- Experience using prototyping to create solutions to simple problems.

Introduction

Most of your programming will be for yourself, but many programmers are writing programs for customers. These customers could be the end users of the program but more often will be a company who is paying the programmer for their work. The name given to this company is the client.

Problems occur where clients do not fully understand programming. Most of them do not or they would not be commissioning the programmer to do the work. But it is their project and communicating the look and feel to the client of what is being developed is critical. This is where prototyping becomes essential.

What is prototyping and what is its purpose?

The concept behind prototyping is to offer people who have an interest in a system the capability of evaluating the system developer's proposed designs, rather than having to interpret those designs based on some other means such as descriptions.

A prototype typically simulates only a few aspects of the final product and at this point may be completely different from the end result.

Key point

The most useful purpose of prototyping is based on providing a simulation of some behaviour or functionality.

Advantages of prototyping

Prototyping offers many advantages within software development. It allows the customer and the developer to assess whether the developed software matches the software specification according to which the program should have been built.

Prototyping can offer improvements to the quality and definition of a client's requirements and improve the specifications provided to developers. Most projects run over budget because the designer and the client do not fully understand what is possible or even wanted. Making a functioning or even non-functioning prototype first often results in faster and less expensive software, and less wasted time.

A fundamental requirement of prototyping is end user involvement. This allows end users to see and interact with a prototype, providing them with an opportunity to offer improvements and more thorough feedback and specifications. The existence of a prototype enabling detailed examination by users prevents misunderstandings and miscommunications that can occur when each side thinks the other understands what they said.

Since users understand the fundamental issues of the problem better than anyone on the development team does, the increased interaction can contribute to a final product that is more likely to satisfy the users' desire for look, feel and performance.

Questions

1 Explain how end users could be involved in evaluating a new computer game.
2 List five of the issues a development company could face by using end users as part of a prototyping process.

Disadvantages of prototyping

Prototyping can also have disadvantages, although these can often be put down to misusing the process of prototyping.

Insufficient analysis

If the parts of the system prototyped are just very small parts of the software, developers can be distracted from properly analysing the complete project. This can result in overlooking much better solutions. Incomplete specifications or even the adaptation of a very limited prototype often results in a poorly engineered final solution.

Sometimes limited prototypes work well on their own but when they are used as the basis for a final product the system is not scalable. This may not be noticed if the developers are too focused on building a prototype as a model.

User confusion of prototype and finished system

There is a risk that users can begin to think that a prototype, which is intended to be discarded, is actually the final system that merely needs to be finished or polished. This can lead to the expectation that the prototype should accurately model the performance of the final system when this is definitely not the intention of the developers.

Users can also become attached to features or functionality that were included in a prototype for consideration and then removed from the specification for the final system, and this can lead to conflict.

Developer attachment to prototype

Developers and programmers also become attached to prototypes that they have spent many hours producing. This can lead to problems like simply trying to turn a limited prototype into a final system. A solution to this problem is to only use what is called throwaway prototyping, where only parts of the system are tested, rather than evolutionary prototyping where the prototype is a fully working system.

Excessive development time of the prototype

Prototyping should be carried out quickly. This prevents the prototype becoming too complex. Good prototyping increases productivity but an unnecessarily complex prototype can hold up the development team and delay the final product.

Expense of implementing prototyping

The cost of producing software prototypes can be very high. Many organisations have existing development methodologies based on past practices and programming languages in place, and making alterations to them can mean retraining. Unfortunately this leads many companies to jump into prototyping using existing skills and without bothering to retrain their workers as much as they should. The costs of not prototyping a large project can work out to be much higher than the cost of the prototype.

A common problem with adopting a good prototyping approach to software development is a high expectation for productivity improvement without sufficient focus on the learning curve in using new software and prototyping techniques.

Task

Explore prototyping and how it is used in both computing and non-computing products.

Question

Discuss the benefits and drawbacks of prototyping a coded solution.

Chapter 18
Application testing

Specification coverage

- Testing coded solutions
- Different kinds of testing
- Test plans
- Practical experience in testing

Learning outcomes

- Understand the need for rigorous testing of coded solutions.
- Understand the different types of tests that can be used, including unit/modular testing.
- You should be able to create suitable test plans and carry out suitable testing to demonstrate your solutions work as intended.
- You should be able to hand test simple code designs/algorithms using trace tables.

Introduction

In general, testing is finding out how well something works. You will be tested in your understanding of computing. In this sense testing finds out what level of knowledge or skill you have acquired.

Software testing is similar. It is much more than just error detection. Testing software is operating the software under controlled conditions to see how well it works.

You will use testing to ensure that the script you have written actually does what it is supposed to do. It is not possible to write scripts perfectly so that they always do exactly what they are supposed to do first time. And even if it were possible, a user would find something that does not work on their machine.

Key point

Testing software is operating the software under controlled conditions to see how well it works.

You will need to test all your scripts in order to locate and fix any errors.

Why do we need to carry out a formal test?

The reason we need to test and document coded solutions is to enable us to make objective judgements about how well a software product meets, exceeds or fails to meet a set of criteria that is normally stated in the specification requirement.

In order to test your own products you must ensure that you have a good clear specification requirement before you start the design phase of your project.

We test applications when we wish to understand and be confident that a software product will do its job well when it is released to the end users.

Testing is important in the development of complex applications as it often indicates the end of the development phase and is also the process that establishes the criteria that a client will use to decide whether to accept or refuse the project.

Application testing usually (but not always) involves executing an application with the purpose of finding errors or bugs within the software.

What are the purposes of testing?

There are two reasons why we test software:

- Testing verifies that the application that has been created and delivered meets the specification criteria that were agreed between the developer and the client.
- Testing manages the risk for both the client and the developer. A testing programme identifies whether an application has been produced to the specified requirements of both the client and developer. The project then shifts into the maintenance part of the software development life cycle.

How do you document your tests?

For most programs, it is practically impossible to *prove* that the program is correct on all machines and systems with any input. What you do need to do is prove that your program works as stated in the specification. You do this by producing a testing document saying how you intend to test the program and then showing the results of these tests.

This documentation is called a test plan, and you should provide one with each program. Remember to list only measurable things in your test plan.

Key point

Test plans must be measurable and quantifiable.

When should testing take place?

If a basic software development life cycle is considered, testing is usually carried out between the development period and the application launch or handover to the client. For you this will be before you pass your finished program to the teacher.

Types of testing

There are three types of testing:

- *Under normal conditions.* The application is tested under normal working conditions and the data that a coded solution is supplied with is within the anticipated range.
- *Under extreme conditions.* The coded solution is provided with data that is within the operating range but at its limits of performance.
- *Error behaviour.* An application or program is provided with data that is outside its limits of performance. These particular tests try to break the application and to investigate if things occur when they shouldn't or don't occur when they should.

Let's imagine that you have designed a web-based application. Let's also say that the specification stated that the application will run on all Windows-based PCs. The first thing to test would be if it runs successfully in the default Windows web browser Internet Explorer. But there are many different versions of Internet Explorer and each works slightly differently. So we need to test the application in all of the current versions of the browser software.

Because the specification does not specify the browser, we now also need to test the application in various versions of Firefox, Google Chrome and any other browser that will run on a PC.

Extreme testing could explore what happens on a mobile browser or a non-PC browser, for example, a Windows mobile device.

What this shows you is how important a detailed and specific specification is. If the specification had said to run on Internet Explorer versions 6 and 7, testing would be much easier and less time consuming.

Now let's look at an example of testing procedures with a database.

Under normal test conditions the database is provided with data that is well within its limits, so for instance if a field has limits of 0 and 50, then in these 'normal condition' tests the results received should be well within that range.

If a database is tested under extreme conditions then data is provided that is at the limits of the field's range, so if a field with the limits of 0 and 50 is tested under 'extreme' conditions then the results that should be received should be either 0 or +50.

Lastly, testing error behaviour involves the field with limits of 0 and 50 being subjected to tests where the returned results should be a negative figure or a figure of 51 or more to understand how the software behaves.

Verification and validation

Within software development, testing is always carried out along with procedures of verification and validation. Quite often you see these two words being used to mean the same thing but this is wrong as they have very different definitions:

- Verification is the testing of whether the software performs against criteria that were decided in advance. So it could be looked on as asking the question: 'Have we built the product correctly?' This is usually carried out using what is called functional testing, where testing activities verify the specific actions or functions of software code relative what was originally expected.
- When we check that an application has been correctly written against a specification that has been agreed with the client it is called validation. So it could be looked on as asking the question: 'Have we built the correct product?' Validation is commonly tested using non-functional testing that may not have any relation to a specific function or user action.

Non-functional testing

Non-functional testing tends to reflect the quality of the product, particularly the suitability of the application from the client's point of view. Non-functional testing of applications tends to look at the application as a whole; in other words, how well the complete system should carry out its purpose.

Below is a selection of examples of non-functional software tests:

- *Load test.* The purpose of this is to investigate software behaviour during increasing system loads; for instance, the number of users who use a piece of software all at the same time.

- *Performance test.* For investigating the processing speed and response time for specific scenarios, usually associated with increasing load; for instance, working out what is the desired performance on the client side of a website, for example, how quickly web pages should appear.
- *Volume test.* The investigation of application behaviour relative to the quantity of the data provided; for instance, the processing of large files.
- *Stress test.* Looking at application behaviour when it is overloaded.
- *Security test.* Testing for unauthorised access, denial of service attacks and so on.
- *Robustness test.* The investigation of an application's response to operating mistakes, bugs and so on.

Unit/modular testing

Unit testing, which is also referred to as component testing, is a software development process where the small parts of an application, called units, are individually and independently investigated to see if they work correctly. Unit testing is often automated but it can also be done manually. Unit testing is part of a method of software development that takes a detailed approach to building a product by means of continual testing and revision.

Developers usually create unit tests as they work on code to ensure that the specific function is working as expected. Commonly, one function of the application might have multiple tests, to catch certain errors within the code. Unit testing alone cannot verify the functionality of an application, but rather is a method to ensure that the building blocks that the program uses work independently of each other.

Defining test criteria

When writing a test plan, there are a variety of methods that can be used for differing testing scenarios. However, in each situation, specific criteria need to be defined and agreed between client and developer.

Pass/fail criteria

When developers carry out tests on code, it is inevitable that some aspects will pass and some will fail. The pass/fail criteria need to be described in clear, unambiguous language and agreed with the client. A process should be defined in advance of the tests to allow the developers to record the problems that occur and also any other issues they think need sorting out.

Pass/fail criteria are sometimes referred to as entry/exit or compliance criteria.

It is common for pass/fail test criteria to be used in the testing of graphical user interfaces (GUIs).

Acceptance criteria

Acceptance testing is a validation test that is carried out to judge whether requirements of a specific criterion or a whole contract have has been successfully achieved. The acceptance criteria should be clearly defined and agreed on between the client and the developer. Acceptance criteria test methods should also be defined and agreed.

Within software engineering, acceptance testing may use black box testing on an application, before it is delivered or commissioned. Black box testing is regarded as a functional test, which is also referred to as application testing, confidence testing or quality assurance testing.

Alpha tests

This kind of testing is commonly applied to off-the-shelf applications and is regularly used as a kind of internal acceptance testing procedure, before the program is put over for beta testing. This type of testing can be simulated or quite often operationally tested by potential clients. An outside independent testing company at the developer's site can also test the application.

Beta tests

Beta testing comes after alpha testing and is viewed as a type of external user acceptance testing. Beta versions of the application are released to a limited group of users who are unconnected with the development team. This particular aspect of testing ensures that when the new software is issued it contains as few faults and bugs as possible.

An example of beta testing could be the testing of an upgrade to an image-manipulation program. First, alpha testing would be done at the software company's site until a specific level of performance had been achieved. After that, and for a limited time, the software company would release an issue of the application to a select group of users for beta testing using the users' own equipment.

Test strategies and test plans

Quite often people think that test strategies and test plans are the same documents. This is incorrect as they are dissimilar and have differing purposes.

It is quite a common practice within small projects for some companies to include a test strategy within the test plan. For larger projects, however, there is usually one general test strategy document and a range of test plans focusing on each phase of testing.

Test strategies

Test strategies contain an account of the testing approach for a software development life cycle. The purpose of the strategy is to inform project managers and developers about a range of key issues relating to the testing process. These include the testing objectives, methods of testing new functionality, details of the total testing time and a description of the resource requirements for the testing environment.

A typical test strategy document of a software company could include:
- Scope and objectives (what exactly is required?).
- Roles and responsibilities (who is responsible for what?).
- Communication and status reporting (how will communication take place, when and in what format?).
- Test deliverability (what tests will take place and against what standards?).
- Industry standards to follow (what rules and standards will be followed?).
- Test automation and tools (how will the tests take place and using what?).
- Testing measurements and metrics (what measurements will be taken?).
- Defect reporting and tracking (how will faults found be recorded/corrected?).
- Change and configuration management (what happens if a change is required?).
- Training plan (how will end users be trained to use the product, for example, are product manuals needed?).

Test strategies usually give an account of how risks for the company relative to an application are lessened by carrying out the tests. The strategies also provide a list of the kind of tests that will be performed and what entry/exit criteria (if any) will apply.

Test plans

Test plans are documents that describe the particular approach to each phase or level of testing of an application. The test plan documentation is usually created by the test manager and concentrates on giving an account of what to test, the method of testing, when to test and who will be responsible for conducting each of the tests. The test plan can be viewed as a detailed account of the test workflow, the anticipated results and expectations.

Large test projects occasionally have one master test plan that is a common document for all the test phases, and each test phase has its own test plan.

Task

Write a detailed test plan for one of your own programs.

Question

Why are test plans important? Describe at least five stages of a test plan.

Chapter 19
Networking

Specification coverage

- Computer networks
- Benefits and issues of networks
- Types of computer networks and their benefits and issues

Learning outcomes

- Understand what a computer network is.
- You should be able to discuss the advantages and disadvantages of using a computer network.
- You should be able to describe and explain the bus, ring and star networking topologies.
- You should be able to discuss the advantages and disadvantages of each of these topologies.

Definition of a computer network

A computer network can be described as two or more computers connected together through a communication medium to form a computer network. The purpose of connecting computers together in a network is to exchange information and data; also, networked computers can use the resources of the other computers.

> **Key point**
>
> The purpose of connecting computers together in a network is to exchange information and data; also, networked computers can use resources of other computers.

There are a number of basic components of computer networks and these are described below.

Servers

These are powerful computers that provide services to the other computers on the network.

Clients

Clients are computers that use the services a server provides. Clients are usually less powerful than the server within a network, although even the largest mainframe can act as a client to a small web server somewhere in the world.

Communication media

The communication medium is the physical connection between the devices on a network. This could be through a cable in an organisation's local network, a wireless signal or the internet.

Network adapter

The network adapter or, as it is often referred to, the network interface card (NIC), is a circuit board that is equipped with the components necessary for sending and receiving data. It is usually plugged into one of the available slots on a computer and a transmission cable is attached to the connector on the NIC.

Resources

Resources refers to any peripheral devices that are available to a client on the network such as printers, fax devices and other network devices. However, the term also refers to data and information.

User

A user is basically any person that uses a client to access resources on the network.

Protocols

The protocols of a network are formal, written rules used for the network communications. They are essentially the languages that computers use to communicate between each other on a network. Protocols are often linked, as the functions of different protocols are complementary to each other and mean that together they can carry out the complete task where on their own they could not. One example of this is TCP (Transmission Control Protocol) and IP (Internet Protocol). They are two totally different procedures that are often linked. They carry out the basic operations of the web. TCP/IP is also used on many local area networks.

Some common protocols

TCP

When information is sent over the internet, it is broken up into smaller pieces called packets. Transmission Control Protocol (TCP) is a way of creating the packets and then putting them back together in the correct order.

IP

Internet Protocol (IP) is the method used in a network to send information and data to the correct address. Every computer on a network has to have its own unique address known as the IP address. But the IP does not make any physical connections between computers, it uses TCP to do this.

Mail protocols

Email requires its own set of protocols for sending and for receiving mail. The most common protocol for sending mail is Simple Mail Transfer Protocol (SMTP). The most common protocol for receiving mail is Post Office Protocol (POP). This has been developing over the years and is now at version 3 so it is called POP3.

SMTP and POP3 use TCP for managing the transmission and delivery of mail across the internet.

Hypertext Transfer Protocol

You will already know that web pages are constructed in Hypertext Markup Language (HTML). An HTML page is transmitted over the web using Hypertext Transfer Protocol (HTTP). This protocol also uses TCP/IP to manage all of the data transmissions.

You may also see HTTPS, which stands for Hypertext Transfer Protocol over Secure Socket Layer (HTTPS). This protocol is generally used when you buy things or bank online. Data is sent in an encrypted form, making it secure. You can tell if this is being used as you will see https in your web browser in front of the page's address.

File Transfer Protocol

File Transfer Protocol (FTP) is designed to copy files from one computer to another over a network. Sometimes it is also used for downloading software, films and music from the web, although HTTP is more commonly used now. You will probably use FTP to upload your own website to a web server.

Networking: for and against

Advantages of computer networks

There are a number of advantages to using networks; these include:

- Files can be shared easily between users over a network.
- Network users can communicate via email, instant messenger and VoIP (Voice Over Internet Protocol).
- Networked computers allow users to share common peripheral resources such as printers, fax machines and modems, saving money.
- Networks allow data to be transmitted to remote areas that are connected within local areas.
- Networks allow users to share software stored in a main system.
- Security in networks is of a high standard. Users cannot see other users' files, unlike on stand-alone machines.
- Site (network) software licenses are less expensive than buying several stand-alone licenses.
- The cost of computing is reduced per user as compared to the development and maintenance of a group of un-networked stand-alone computers.
- Within networks, it is much more straightforward to back up data as it is all stored on a file server.

Disadvantages of computer networks

There are also a number of disadvantages to using networks, which include:

- If a virus gets into the system it can spread easily to other computers.
- In the event of a file server breaking down, the files stored on the server become inaccessible. Email may still work if it is stored on a separate email server. The client computers can still be used but they are isolated.
- The cost of purchasing cabling to construct a network and the file servers can be high.
- The management of a large network is complicated, it requires training and a specialist network manager usually needs to be employed.
- With networks there is a risk of hacking, particularly with wide area networks. Stringent security measures are required such as a firewall.

Network topologies

Bus topology

Bus networks, which have absolutely nothing to do with the system bus of a computer, use a common backbone to connect all devices.

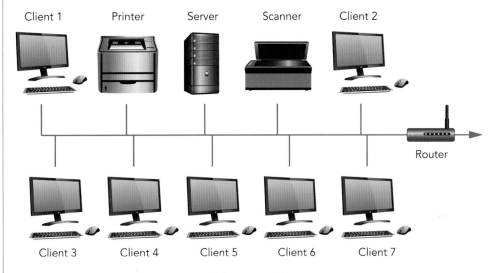

A bus network.

A single cable that functions as the backbone of the network acts as a shared communication medium that devices connect to using an interface connector. When a device wants to communicate with another network device, it transmits a broadcast message along the backbone wire that all the devices see; however, only the intended device actually accepts and processes the message.

Bus topologies are easy to install and only require a relatively small amount of cabling compared to the other topologies. Bus networks are the best choice of topology when the network has only a few devices. If the network grows so that there are more than a few dozen computers connected to the backbone bus, then it is probable that there will be performance issues. Finally, if the backbone cable suffers a catastrophic failure, then the entire network effectively becomes unusable.

Advantages of the bus topology:
- It is easy and cheap to install as a consequence of requiring only a short quantity of cable.
- It is suitable for small networks.

Disadvantages of the bus topology:
- The limited cable length restricts the number of devices that can be connected to the network.

■ This network topology performs well only for a limited number of computers. As more devices are connected, the performance of the network becomes slower as a consequence of data collisions.

Ring topology

When every device has exactly two neighbours for communication purposes the network layout is referred to as a ring topology.

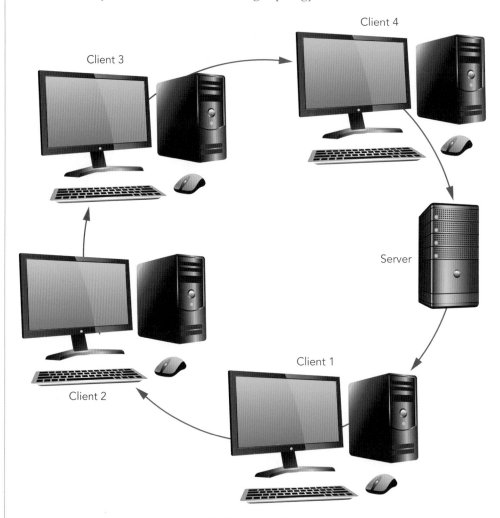

A ring network.

In the ring topology, all messages pass around in the same direction. This can be either clockwise or anticlockwise. As with the bus topology, should a failure in any cable occur or, in this case, a device break down in the ring, it can halt the entire network. Ring topologies are found in some offices and schools.

Advantages of the ring topology:

■ Messages being sent between two workstations pass through all the intermediate devices, resulting in a central server not being required for the management of this topology.

Disadvantages of the ring topology:

- The failure of any cable within the network can cause the entire network to crash.
- Alterations, maintenance or changes being made to the network nodes can affect the performance of the whole network.

Star topology

The star topology is the most familiar topology to most people, as nearly all home networks use the star topology. The star network has a central connection point referred to as a hub node that could be a device such as a network hub, switch or router.

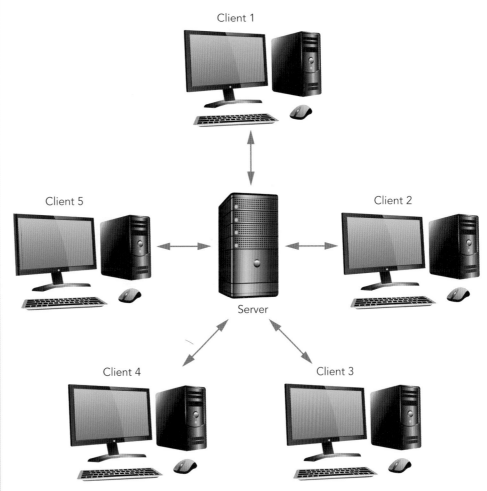

A star network.

A star network generally requires more cable than bus topologies. However, a failure in any star network cable will only restrict access to the computer that is connected using that cable and not the entire network. It should be realised, however, that if the hub fails, the entire network also goes down.

Advantages of the star topology:

- Operational simplicity.
- Allows isolation of each device within the network.

Disadvantages of the star topology:

- The network operation ultimately relies on the correct functioning of the central hub. So, if the central hub crashes it will lead to the failure of the whole network.

Task

List five organisations that use computer networks.

Question

Compare the benefits and drawbacks of star and ring networks.

Wireless networks

Router

A wireless network.

A wireless network (WiFi) and a portable personal router (MiFi) use radio waves to communicate. Radios, mobile phones and televisions use radio waves as well.

This is what happens. A computer's wireless adapter translates data into a radio signal and transmits it using an antenna. It also receives radio signals and converts them into data (remember data has to be zeros and ones).

A wireless modem called a router (WiFi and MiFi) handles the two-way communication. It either receives the data from your computer's wireless adapter or receives data from the internet. In either case it decodes it before passing it on either to the internet server if it is from your computer or to your computer if it is from the internet server.

The router is usually connected by a physical, ethernet connection, but a MiFi uses wireless networks to connect to the internet servers.

Task

Explore developments in MiFi speeds.

Question

Describe the benefits and drawbacks of using wireless rather than wired networks.

Chapter 20
Client server

Introduction

We have looked at how a network uses a client and a server to link computers, but it is not only in networks that use wires where this model works. You may think that you are not on a network but as soon as you switch on your mobile or connect to the internet you are. You become a client. Client–server models don't stop there, they work within programs and even applications. If you think about a web browser discussed in an earlier chapter, the browser software draws its data including words, images, video and more from the web server that is another computer on the internet. You are a client of the web server.

We have also explored cloud computing which is built on a client–server model. With the expansion of these types of services it is very important that you understand the client–server term and how a client system works.

An explanation of the client–server model on mobiles

We have seen how the client–server model is simply a term that defines the connection between two computer programs. We also know that within this model there is always one program, called a client, that requests a service or a resource from another program, called the server, which then fulfils the request.

Key point

Within any network, the client–server model is a very efficient way of connecting applications that are 'distributed' effectively across different locations.

Computer relationships using the client–server model are very common. For example, you want to check the details for a music concert in Birmingham and you type a query into your computer. A client program in your computer sends a request to a server program at the concert venue. That program on the concert venue server will, in turn, forward the request to its own client program which then sends a request to a database server to retrieve all the details of your requested concert. The dates, times and price of the tickets are then returned to the venue server, which then sends the information back to the client in your personal computer, which presents the information to you on your monitor or smartphone screen.

These days, it is fair to say that almost all modern business programs use the client–server model; however, what is also interesting is that the internet's main program, TCP/IP, also uses this model.

There are other program relationship models in use and these include:

■ master–slave: where one program is in charge of all other programs
■ peer to peer: where either of the two programs is able to initiate a transaction.

Question

Explain how a smartphone relies on a client–server model to work.

Handshaking

Handshaking.

When we meet someone in business we shake their hand as a greeting. This is true in computing too: when two computers connect in a network they first use a handshake.

For computers to work together they have to use what are called protocols. A protocol is a set of rules that governs the transfer of data between computers. Protocols are essential for any communication between computers and networks. They determine the speed of transmission, size of bytes, error-checking methods and even whether communication will be asynchronous or synchronous. Examples of protocols are token ring and TCP/IP. They are the methods by which all networked computers set up a link through some kind of networking equipment.

Handshaking establishes which protocols to use and controls the flow of data between the two or more connected computers. All network connections, such as a request from a web browser to a web server, or a file-sharing connection between peer-to-peer computers, have their own handshaking protocols, which must be completed before finishing the action requested by the user.

The handshaking process usually occurs when a computer is about to communicate with what is called a foreign device to establish the rules for communication.

The diagram below shows a three-way handshake via TCP/IP.

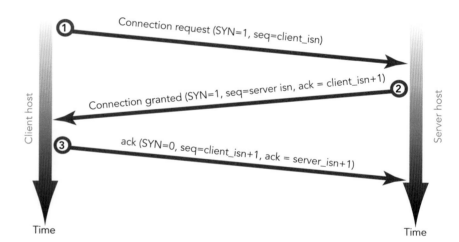

1 A request to connect is sent.
2 A connection is granted.
3 Protocol parameters are agreed.

During handshaking, the protocol parameters, which both the communicating devices and systems understand, are negotiated. As we have seen, these parameters include things such as coding issues, information transfer rate and interruption procedures.

Key term

Asynchronous is where an action, data or communication occurs randomly and therefore not at regular intervals, whereas synchronous actions, data or communications happen at regular intervals. An example outside computing would be synchronised swimming. Everyone does the same actions at exactly the same time (synchronously) with the music, whereas in a normal swimming session everyone does their own thing in an asynchronous and rather chaotic way with no real pattern. When you text or talk to someone on a mobile you have an asynchronous communication as you send your text, wait for a reply or for an undefined amount of time and then send the next text. As most communication between computers and peripherals like printers is also asynchronous, the computer has to add bit code at the start and stop of each sequence, so this type of communication is often called start–stop transmission in computing or start–stop communication.

Key point

The handshaking process usually occurs when a computer is about to communicate with what is called a foreign device to establish the rules for communication.

Every communication system has five basic needs/requirements:

- a data source (this is where the data originates)
- a transmitter (a device that will be used to transmit data from its source)
- a transmission medium (cables or another data transfer method)
- a receiver (a device used to receive data)
- a destination (where the data will be placed or displayed).

Question

Discuss the term 'handshake' and say why it is used in computing.

Transmitting the data

Any network is governed by the speed that data can travel. If you imagine the cables, wireless connections or systems to be a motorway network, the roads have width and speed limits and can get slow if there are too many cars travelling at the same time or the motorway is full of large vehicles like lorries. This works the same with networks. When discussing network protocols you will often see the following terms used:

- *Bandwidth*. This is the amount of data which can be transmitted on a medium (wires or wireless) over a fixed period of time (over a second). It is measured using bits per second or baud. Bits per second (bps) is therefore a measure of transmission speed, the number of bits (zeros or ones) that can be transmitted in a second.
- *Baud rate*. This is a measure of how fast a change of state occurs (that is, a change from zero to one).

Data packets

Anything sent between computers or programs has to be divided up into what are called packets. Even a PowerPoint file or spreadsheet has to be divided into packets to be transmitted. Imagine an object built of LEGO where each brick is a packet. Packets are small data units. Of course, once transmitted the packets have to be put back together in the correct order. In computing, the Open System Interconnection (OSI) model looks after this. OSI is not one protocol, it is a collection of protocols. These protocols wrap each data packet with a set of instructions. The computing name for this is encapsulation. Once all the

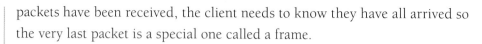

packets have been received, the client needs to know they have all arrived so the very last packet is a special one called a frame.

To demonstrate the handshaking process, here is a simple example that could involve the receiver sending a message indicating:

```
"I received your last message and I am ready for you to
send me another one."
```

A more complex handshaking scenario could involve the receiver replying with a negative acknowledgement (because the message was not received due to a crash or corruption) indicating:

```
"I did not receive your last message correctly, please
resend it."
```

Question

Discuss the term 'data packet' and say why it is used in computing.

Differences between client-side and server-side programming

It is important to know the difference between client-side programming and server-side programming. As we have seen, client-side programming is run on the client machine. An example of client-side programming is JavaScript. Server-side programming is run on the remote server. Some examples of server-side programming languages are PHP, C# and .NET.

Chapter 21
Web application concepts

Specification coverage
■ Knowledge of server- and client-side coding.

Learning outcomes
■ Understand the concept of coding at the server and client end.
■ Know what can be coded at the server end.
■ Know what can be coded at the client end.
■ You should have experience of coding solutions to simple web application problems.

Introduction

Whenever you use a network that is not peer to peer, you are involved in what is called a client–server model. One machine is the server and the other is the client.

What you may not realise is that when you go on to the internet you are on a client–server network too. You see the web pages displayed in your own browser. They are not on your own computer or mobile. These pages are stored on a web server, which is not the same thing as your web browser. The web server can be located anywhere in the world; your web browser is on your own computer. The web browser interprets code that is sent to it from the web server and turns it into a web page. The code will mainly be HTML, but will probably also contain elements of JavaScript, Flash movies and more.

In this book we have been exploring PHP as a programming language. PHP is a server-side programming language; this means that it runs on the server, not on your machine. Yet you know that PHP can be run within HTML and can also contain JavaScript code, so we have server side and software code on your machine running together to make the application work.

You are a customer of the web server; you are in computing terms called a client.

Key term

Even on the internet you are in a client–server model. The place where the code is stored is called a web server and you are the client.

Advantages and disadvantages of a client–server model

Before we explore this in more detail, let us look at a few of the benefits and drawbacks of any network using a client–server model.

Advantages of client–server networks

- All the files are stored at the same place. In this way, finding files and file management is easy.
- As new information is uploaded to a server database, each workstation does not need to have its own storage capacities increased.
- Back-up and recovery are much simpler and often automatic.
- Everything is centralised and managed in one place. Access rights and resource allocation are all done by servers.
- Improved accessibility from various platforms in the network means that the server can be accessed remotely across different devices.
- Server-side security is much more robust.
- Updates, new resources and systems can be added by making necessary changes in the server.

Disadvantages of client–server networks

- Congestion in the network. Too many requests from clients may lead to congestion.
- If you are downloading a file from the server and it gets abandoned due to some error, download stops altogether.
- It is very expensive to install and manage this type of computing.
- You need professional IT people to maintain the servers and network.

It is interesting to note that some of the disadvantages of client–server networks become advantages in a cloud-based network where maintenance is externally provided and the costs of installation reduce significantly.

How does it all work over the internet?

Your computer or an application on your mobile asks for the web page and some of the code is sent back to you, the client. The application on your mobile device or desktop provides some functionality to you but this is in conjunction with the server on the internet.

If you are using a web browser it will retrieve documents from servers around the world. You can connect to FTP servers if you want to upload or download files.

Wireless clients connecting to a web server.

When you are on the internet, most of the time the web server will just send you the code, but web servers can also manipulate code within a web page before sending it to the client. To do this the web server executes a program on the server before sending the pages. The name given to this is 'server-side' programming.

Other applications that use a peer-to-peer network can also be modelled as client–server applications, with either peer taking the role of the client or the server, depending on the task.

The server-side program can be written in a variety of languages. Some of the programming languages and technologies that can be used are PHP, ASP (Active Server Pages), C/C++ and JSP (Java Server Pages not JavaScript). There are others but to run the server must support the chosen server-side language. Code executed on the web server is called server-side code. If code is executed on your browser, it is called client-side code.

What is done server side?

There are a number of actions that can be programmed on the server. One of the main functions that requires server-side code is to build pages customised for the type of browser that requested a page. Movies, for example, require different versions according to the browser being used. Server-side code can also draw information from a database to create information for a web page. Anything that requires information from a database, such as the number of people on the server, their address and any type of analytical information, has to be done on the server side. A visitor counter is usually a server-side program.

Modern developments in programming are blurring some aspects of client–server programming. As internet speeds get faster and more reliable, things like counters can use client-side scripting using jquery, which runs on the client side but accesses a database on the server side.

Key point

Web programmers like server-side scripts such as PHP as they are more secure than client-side code. You cannot easily download and steal the code if it is server side.

What is done client side?

Client-side programming is important because the client and the server are not always connected. The browser is separate from the server. By including code within the web page, a number of features can be added. This is also a much quicker way to execute code even if the client and server are connected, as the communications between parts of your computer are much faster than any internet connection.

Key point

HTML, Flash, JavaScript, ActiveX controls and a number of other technologies can be executed on the client side. You can execute any technology supported by your browser.

Security

Server-side coded scripts are much more secure than client-side scripts. Online shops have to use server-side scripting for online payments. When a user accesses their bank account online, the server-side script communicates with the client-side script using encryption. It would be far too insecure to use the plain text that runs on the client-side browser. Hackers would easily view the code and steal private information from the user's computer. Many web-based games run on the server side for the same reason. The programmer needs to make sure players cannot modify the data and hack into the game code.

Task

List the advantages and disadvantages of a client–server model when used over the internet.

Gaming

Flash-based games are delivered from the cloud-based servers but run client side. But multi-player games and any game that remembers scores across players have to also be driven server side.

Most modern games use client-side detection. You carry out an action and then your system sends data packets to the game server. But this is changing: some of the very latest games even use server-side rendering. The client browser is only used as a canvas. This enables the game designer to create 3D worlds and unique gaming experiences. But the main advantage of server-side rendering is when it is used for mobile gaming. As we discovered in earlier chapters, mobiles cannot have the large graphics processors that can be put into larger computers. By using server-side programming, the games can draw on cloud-based high-end graphics cards.

Web application

A web application is a server-side application that can be used by accessing a web server through the internet or an intranet. The browser is used as a 'thin' client.

This type of application has become very popular due to the ability of the programmers to update and maintain web applications without the end users needing to update the software on their own machines.

Question

Briefly describe the term client–server model, stating how it benefits the company and customer.

Chapter 22
Use of external code sources

Learning outcomes
- You should know of the existence of external code sources.
- You should know how to integrate code from these sources into your own code.
- You should be able to explain the advantages and disadvantages of using such sources.

Introduction

New developments in web programming led to people starting to do the same thing. They started to use data and code from lots of external places to create something unique. They created a web mashup.

Mashups

A web mashup is simply a web page or coded application used to combine data or functionality from two or more sources to create a new product.

When Google released some of its map code as an Application Programming Interface or API, web developers were able to integrate mapping into their own applications without developing all the code themselves.

Today there are lots of video and photo hosting sites sharing part of their code with APIs, including Flickr, Yahoo and YouTube. Other APIs quickly followed such as PayPal, Twitter, Facebook, price comparison tools for online shopping and multi-site searches.

Programmers were now able to integrate code from these external sources into their own code. They simply used external code, web feeds, JavaScript and widgets.

Key term

API stands for Application Programming Interface. The key word is *interface*. An interface is a common boundary between two separate systems. It is the way that codes on two different systems can communicate with each other.

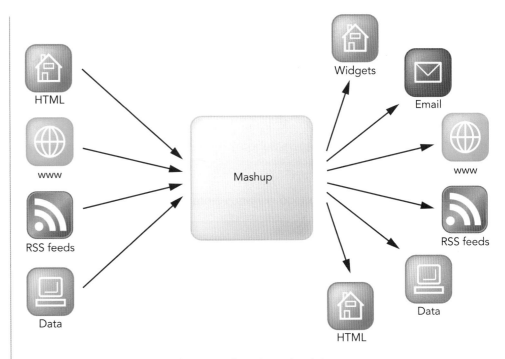

Sharing and reusing others' data.

Mashups can be used by users too. Using a mashup they can combine information on their interests from other sources such as Google, YouTube and Yahoo into one interface.

Questions

1 Why would a photo-sharing site want to share its API?
2 Describe three benefits to a web developer of creating a mashup rather than writing all the code for themselves.

What is iframe?

An iframe (inline frame) is an HTML document embedded inside another HTML document on a website. An iframe can be configured with its own scrollbar independent of the surrounding page's scrollbar. To the user they are still on the same site but in reality they have embedded content and programming from another source. The user does not have to reload the surrounding page.

The iframe often uses JavaScript but it is designed to embed interactive applications in web pages which could be either client or server side.

Question

Describe the main benefits to a website designer of using iframe.

What is an API?

APIs are carefully coded to expose only chosen functionality and/or data to third parties who want to use the external functionality and code. They have to also safeguard other parts of the application.

APIs are invisible to the end user; they run silently in the background. They have been designed to provide a channel for applications to work with each other to make sure the client gets the required functionality and information.

Task

Research the term API and list at least three major companies that provide their API for integration into other organisations' products. You should start with Google Maps and PayPal.

Question

Describe three benefits to a provider of an online education platform of providing other companies with its API.

Putting our knowledge together

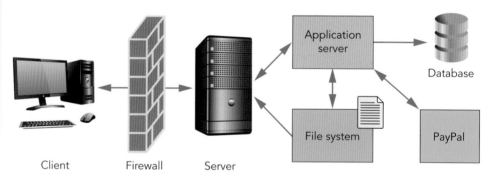

A mashup at work using PayPal's API.

How it all works in practice

Let's put some of our knowledge from earlier chapters together. A user (client side) visits a website (Film4U) which supplies on-demand films. The user needs to sign up on the site and so passes through the firewall used to protect security on the client and access the Film4U web server. They enter their details and these are placed in a database linked to the applications server using SQL. Once the user has registered, each time they visit the site they view the content delivered by the file server and view it in their web browser. They log into their account by putting their details into a form in their browser which is really an iframe that is server side. It checks their details via the applications server in the database using SQL and logs them into the system.

Users view the trailers for a few films which are Flash based and run in their browsers client side delivered by the file system. Then they decide to buy credit to watch a film. They click 'buy film' in the browser and it routes them, again using an iframe, to the payment gateway at PayPal, which is linked to the application server. The users pay using the secure service on the PayPal payment gateway and then they are returned to the Film4U server. It receives what is called a token from PayPal and so adds the successful purchase to the file in its relational database. Now the user will be given access to the file server where the film they have paid for is stored and they will be able to watch it in their browser.

At all times they will be in their own browser, and they will not notice all the things that are happening across servers. All the handshakes are made possible by external code sources on the various servers via the APIs and iframes, all invisible to the user.

Are APIs hard to use?

Companies such as PayPal want people to use their external code so the API is well documented. But as with all code, each programmer has their own way of writing a program and it can be quite hard to get inside the head of the original programmer to integrate code.

SaaS

Building on the idea of APIs is embedding whole applications into a platform. SaaS stands for Software as a Service. SaaS is not a completely new idea: users of webmail services such as Hotmail have used SaaS for some time. The software sends, reads and organises emails, not on the user's machine, but via their web browser.

Chapter 23
Database concepts

Specification coverage

- Concepts of relational databases

Learning outcomes

- Understand the basic concepts of a relational database as a data store.
- You should be able to explain the terms: record, field, table, query, primary key, relationship, index and search criteria.

Introduction

All businesses have data that needs to be gathered, collated and analysed, and a relational database satisfies these requirements.

Relational databases can be used to look after business data.

The ability to share data including documents, images and customer details with employees across the company is also vitally important. Databases are at the heart of any cloud-based system as well.

> ### Task
> Research database uses in today's cloud-based world and describe three uses in detail.

Let's look at what a database does.

What is a database?

Databases use a series of tables to store data. A table simply refers to a two-dimensional representation of data stored in rows and columns. For example:

Steve	Cushing	steve@example.com
John	Wilson	john@example.com
Jess	Hadden	jess@example.com

So we have a table with rows containing a person's details and columns.

Each table needs a unique name so that the database management system (often referred to as the DBMS) can find the correct table. We will call this table 'contacts'. Next, each column needs a name.

first_name	last_name	email_address
Steve	Cushing	steve@example.com
John	Wilson	john@example.com
Jess	Hadden	jess@example.com

To make the database usable we need to add a unique key to the table. Most database developers create their own column with a computer-generated unique number to act as the unique key, referred to as the databases key field.

first_name	last_name	email_address	key
Steve	Cushing	steve@example.com	1001
John	Wilson	john@example.com	1002
Jess	Hadden	jess@example.com	1003

We could just keep adding fields for any additional data. This would be called a flat file database, but these can be very slow to use, so most professional databases have different tables linked together. Let's look at how that works.

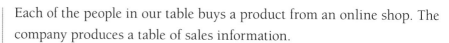

Each of the people in our table buys a product from an online shop. The company produces a table of sales information.

number	product_name	product_code	item_id
10	Rise and Fall	B067	1010
2	Times Square	H766	1020
1	Home	L678	1030

So now we need to link the two tables together, to relate the data in one table with another. This is where the relational database gets its name. A link table like the one below is used.

item_id	key
1010	1001
1020	1002
1030	1003

By referring to the link table you can see that Jess Hadden purchased one copy of the product L678 Home.

Sometimes in data tables the *item_id* and *key* are the same. What then happens to the unique key field? In relational databases nothing is unique in combined tables. The second key is called a foreign key which means that the number used in a foreign key column is not necessarily unique to the linked table but it must be unique to the table it is referring to.

Question

What is the difference between a key field in a flat file database and a key field in a relational database?

In addition to the comprehensive functionality of a relational database, there is a need to not only develop but also maintain the database. IT personnel such as data analysts, database designers and database administrators all need to be able to modify the data within a database to produce useful information for both day-to-day organisational activities and long-term planning.

Databases are like spreadsheets ... aren't they?

Most of us are all familiar with spreadsheets. We find them simple to create and they are often used in schools much like a database. Let's analyse the features and functionality of spreadsheets to investigate how good a database tool they actually are.

In a similar way to databases, spreadsheets are frequently used to capture and store information in tables. They have the capability to link table cells on one worksheet to those on another worksheet, and can specify that data be entered in a particular cell in a particular format. It is also a simple operation to calculate formulas from a group of cells on the spreadsheet, create charts, and process data in other ways.

Having said this, there are many areas in which spreadsheets are nothing like a database and this table highlights these:

Spreadsheets	Databases
Cells can be formatted as a formula	Database columns have a fixed value
A number of different data types can be stored in a column of a spreadsheet	In a column of a database only a single data type can be stored
Accessible to only one user at any one time	Accessible to a multiple of users at any time as well as offering a choice of 'read and write' permissions across various areas of a database
Corrupted spreadsheets cannot usually be repaired	There is a range of tools for repairing databases
There is no way of making a row (record) unique	Individual rows within databases have the capability to be identified by a unique 'primary key'

Relational databases

As we have seen, a relational database is a group of data items assembled into a set of formatted tables from which data can be searched, accessed and interrogated in a multitude of different ways without having to reorganise the database tables.

Key point

The standard user interface to any relational database is the Structured Query Language (SQL). By using SQL statements, interactive queries for information can be made for the purpose of retrieving information from a relational database and for gathering data for reports.

As well as being quite simple to create and access, a relational database has the significant benefit of being relatively straightforward to extend. After the original database has been produced, a new data category can be included without the need to modify all the existing applications as new tables can be added and linked.

As already mentioned, relational databases are a set of tables consisting of data organised into predefined categories. The tables, which are sometimes referred to as *relations*, comprise one or more categories that are arranged into columns. Each row contains a unique instance of data for the categories defined by the columns.

Databases can be designed so that different users see a different view of the database that is customised to suit the individual user's needs. For example, a sales manager may wish to view a report on all customers that had bought products after a certain date, whereas a finance manager within the same company could, from the same database, acquire a report on accounts that needed to be paid.

This is achieved by simply relating the tables needed by that user.

> ## Question ❓
>
> Describe three of the main differences between spreadsheets and databases.

Components of relational databases

The foundation for any relational database management system (RDBMS) is the relational model and this has three basic components:

- a store
- a method of creating and retrieving data
- a method of ensuring that the data is logically consistent.

Let's look at the fundamental components of a traditional relational database system and how it is designed.

Tables

A table in a relational database is also referred to as a 'relation'. It is a two-dimensional structure used to store related information. A relational database consists of two or more related tables.

Records

In databases, records are a complete single set of information. Records are comprised of fields (see below). A set of records constitutes a file. For example, a personnel file of employees may contain records that have seven fields, such as age, gender, house number, street name, town, telephone number, National Insurance number and so on.

Rows

A row within a 'relation' table is an instance of one record, such as one employee and their respective details that are contained within the fields of the records.

Columns

Columns within a database table contain all the information of a single type, such as all employees' names, all of the phone numbers or all the address details. As part of the validation and verification of the information, columns are usually formatted to accept certain types of data such as integers, Boolean, decimals (to a stated number of decimal places) or strings.

Field

Within relational database tables, a field is a single snippet of data that is at the intersection of a row and a column. It is the smallest piece of information that can be retrieved using the database's SQL and forms part of an individual record.

Queries

A database query is fundamentally a question that you put to the database. The outcome of the query is the information that is returned by the database in answer to the question. Queries are created using SQL, which looks like a high-level programming language.

Question

Describe three of the main benefits to a company of using a relational database over a flat file database or spreadsheet used to store the same customer data.

Primary keys

Every relational database should contain one or more columns that are assigned as the primary key. The important and crucial factor for the primary key to work is that the value it holds must be unique for each of the records contained within the table.

Key point

The important and crucial factor for the primary key to work is that the value it holds must be unique for each of the records contained within the table.

If we take our personnel database example referred to earlier, we know that it contains personal information on all our organisation's employees.

Now, we need to choose a suitable column of information, where each field within that column can uniquely identify each employee's record, which can act as our primary key. So why don't we choose the column containing the employee's surname?

Well, this would not work correctly because there may be two or more people working within the business called Jones, Davies or Smith. The same problem would occur if we used the column containing first names or street titles. You could use National Insurance numbers; however, their use is quite controversial as a consequence of certain privacy issues. A better idea would be to create a column with unique employee identifiers and, these days, this is what most companies do.

When the primary key has been selected and built into the database, the database management system will ensure the uniqueness of the key, so that should you attempt to add a duplicate record with a key that already exists within the table the system will disallow the addition and present you with a warning window.

Relationships

Database relationships work by comparing data in key fields. This occurs between fields that have corresponding names in both tables. In almost all cases, the fields contain the primary key for one of the tables, which then supplies the unique identifier for each record and the 'foreign' key in the other table. The foreign key is a column identified to establish a connection between the data in two tables.

A link is established between two tables by adding the column that holds the primary key in the first table to the other table. The duplicated column within the second table then becomes the foreign key.

Although the most important responsibility of a foreign key is to manage the data that is stored in the foreign key table, it additionally manages changes to data in the primary key table. The link between the two tables ensures that data integrity is maintained between the two tables by ensuring that alterations cannot occur to data in the primary key table, if the alterations undermine the link to the data in the foreign key table.

If someone tries to delete the record row in a primary key table or to alter a primary key value, an error will occur if it is linked to a foreign key value in another table. In order to carry out a successful alteration or deletion to a record in a foreign key table, initially, you should either delete or alter the

Key term

Database relationships work by comparing data in key fields.

foreign key data contained within the second table, thereby linking the foreign key to different primary key data.

Index

Database indexes assist database management systems to find and sort records more quickly. It is really important that when you produce a database, you should also create indexes for the columns used in queries to find data.

Indexes in databases can be compared to indexes in books. If you look at a book's index, it enables you to find the information you want quickly without having to read through the entire book. Within a database, the index enables the database software to search for and find data in a table without having to scan the whole table.

Indexes can be based on a single field or on multiple fields. Indexes that use a number of fields enable the user to distinguish between records in which the first field may have the same value.

Even though indexes greatly improve the efficiency of a database, tables that possess indexes need more storage space within the database. Also, the commands that insert, update or delete data within databases need more processing time.

When choosing the fields to use for indexes you should consider using fields you search frequently, or fields you sort regularly, or fields that you combine frequently with fields in other tables when queries are created. If a large number of the values within a field are identical, then an index might not significantly improve the speed of queries.

Key point

Primary keys within tables are automatically indexed.

Question

Describe briefly the term index when used in the context of a relational database.

Chapter 24
Query methods (SQL)

Specification coverage
- Understand SQL concepts
- Create SQL statements

Learning outcomes
- You should be able to create simple SQL statements to extract, add and edit data stored in databases.
- You should have experience of using these SQL statements from within your own coded systems.

Introduction

SQL (Structured Query Language) databases were discussed earlier in the book when we looked at external data sources. We used the command term 'query' to explore an SQL database. All SQL code is written in the form of a query statement and this is 'executed' against a database.

SQL queries perform some types of data operation that could be selecting, inserting/updating, or creating what are called data objects.

We explored how every query statement begins with a clause such as DELETE, CREATE, SELECT or UPDATE.

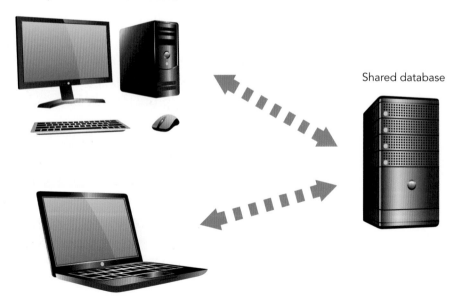

Shared database

Querying a database. Why is that a useful thing to do?

SQL databases can be created on a single machine but often large databases are shared between users. This is achieved by installing them on a dedicated server.

Now that you understand databases in more detail we should revisit SQL and how it would work in our relational database.

Question

Describe briefly three benefits to an online company of using an SQL database.

Creating a table

To create the first table in Chapter 23 using SQL we need to create a table called contacts with first_name, last_name and email_address plus a key.

The SQL command for creating a table is easy, it is CREATE TABLE. So our code would look like this:

```
CREATE TABLE contacts (
    first_name CHAR (30) NULL ,
    last_name CHAR (40) NULL ,
    email_address VARCHAR (80) NULL
    key INT IDENTITY (1001, 1) NOT NULL ,
    );
```

If you look at the code most of it should make sense to you.

We are stating that first_name is a character column (CHAR) that will store 30 or fewer characters in it. We are also saying the first_name can be empty using the NULL statement. The last_name field is similar but can have 40 characters.

Key point

The key field in a database must always have a NOT NULL statement as it must always have a value.

The email_address field uses VARCHAR, which stores a set of alphanumeric characters in a variable string. We could have used CHAR but this command allocates memory space to the stated length, so the last_name command will allocate 40 spaces even if the last name is really short. In some, but not all systems, the VARCHAR will use less memory as it is a variable and will only store the number of characters used. I say *some* systems because there could be a minimum length.

The line for the key uses the term INT as we want it to be an integer; the next part of the code shows that we want it to start with 1001 and go up in increments of 1. Notice also the use of NOT NULL as we must have a key number to make our relational database work.

> **Key point**
>
> The semicolon at the end of a statement tells the database system that you have finished the command.

So now we have a table but so far it has no data. To add data we need to use the command INSERT INTO.

> **Task**
>
> Create a table using SQL with the following fields: first_name, last_name, telephone, email_address, id, where the id is the unique identifier.

The SQL INSERT INTO statement

The SQL INSERT INTO statement is used to insert a new row in a database table. Let's have a look at the syntax of the function. There are two methods of writing the INSERT INTO statement. In the first method, we do not specify the column names where the data will be inserted, only their values:

```
INSERT INTO table_name
VALUES (value1, value2, value3,...)
```

In the second method, both the column names and the values to be inserted are specified:

```
INSERT INTO table_name (column1, column2, column3,...)
VALUES (value1, value2, value3,...)
```

So we have our table called contents and we know how to insert data. Now let's add the first record:

```
INSERT INTO contacts (first_name,
   last_name,
   email_address)
 VALUES ('Steve',
   'Cushing',
   'steve@example.com');
```

Key point

You must add data in the same order as the rows in your table. If you do not know the data, for example if Steve Cushing did not have an email address, you would add NULL.

```
INSERT INTO contacts (first_name,
    last_name,
    email_address)
VALUES ('Steve',
    'Cushing',
    NULL);
```

The SQL UPDATE statement

What happens if a user changes their email address? What we need to do is UPDATE the field. The UPDATE statement is used to edit existing records in a table. Let's take a look at the syntax of the UPDATE statement:

```
UPDATE table_name
SET column1=value, column2=value2,...
WHERE some_column=some_value
```

It is worth taking note of the WHERE clause, which specifies which record or records should be updated. If the WHERE clause is left out, then all records will be edited.

Let's change Steve Cushing's email address in our database:

```
UPDATE contacts
    SET email_address = 'scushing@example.org'
WHERE contact_id = 1001;
```

Notice the use of the SET command: this changes a row in the database table. You can add lots of changes to a row in the database using the SET command if you separate each column change with a comma.

Task

Add your own personal data to your table using SQL. You should add your name, telephone number and email address to the correct fields and add a unique identifier starting with 5002 with each increment being 2.

Other important commands

The SELECT command is used to tell the database system what you want to find in a table but you must say what data you want from a column. If you want all the columns you would use SELECT *.

In SQL, the SELECT statement is used to choose data from a database. Let's have a look at the syntax of the statement:

```
SELECT column_name(s)
FROM table_name
```

and

```
SELECT * FROM table_name
```

WHERE commands select only the data stated in the command, so:

```
SELECT first_name, email_address
    FROM contacts
    WHERE first_name = 'Steve';
```

will only find people with the first_name Steve.

Task

Add the details of five friends to your SQL database then sort by second name.

Sorting

So what if we want to sort the data in our database?

```
SELECT *
    FROM contacts
    ORDER BY last_name DESC;
```

will sort the data by last_name in DESCending order.

Deleting

And what if we want to delete a customer in our data table?

```
DELETE FROM contacts
WHERE key = 1003;
```

In this case DELETE removes the row in table 'contacts' where the key is equal to 1003. That means Jess Hadden will no longer be in our database.

Task

Delete one of the contacts in your database.

There are a number of very useful operators that you can use to make comparisons and filter data. Keep in mind, though, each database management system can be different and the operators they use can change from one system to another.

The table shows some of the most common operators.

Operator	The operator compares data
=	to see if it is equal
<>	to see if it is not equal
<	to see if the data is less than your criteria
<=	to see if the data is less than or equal to your criteria
>	to see if the data is greater than your criteria
>=	to see if the data is greater than or equal to your criteria
IS NULL	to make sure that there is no data in the column

Chapter 25
Connecting to databases from applications and web-based apps

Introduction

Web-based databases are at the core of developments in cloud-based technology. Let's look at some specific examples:

- A blogging site always stores old articles in a database.
- All banking sites use online databases to allow you access to your account information.
- Online shops all use databases both for products and to store user information.

So, how can you use a database with your own web-based applications? There are many different programming languages that you could use. We have already explored two of them: SQL and PHP. Some of the more notable others would include ASP, ASP.NET, Perl and JSP. Each has its own advantages and disadvantages.

These are examples of the types of project you could undertake:

- A friend's database that can be accessed from your website.
- A list of friends' and family photographs that can be downloaded.
- A schedule of events for your school or college activities.

Distributed applications

By storing data in web-based databases, new web technologies have led to what are called distributed applications. Distributed application programs have many parts that are stored on different virtual machines. The different virtual machines can be on the same or even different systems. This, for example, allows smartphones to access the same resources as desktops.

Computing is said to be distributed when the computer programming and data that computers work on are spread out over more than one computer, usually over a network. We explored client–server models in Chapter 20 and these are at the core of distributed applications.

All distributed applications run on two or more computers in a network. In the client–server environment we studied in Chapter 20, distributed applications had two parts:

- the client at what is called the 'front end' that needs minimal computer resources
- the server called the 'back end' that requires large amounts of power and often specialised hardware.

Question

What are the advantages to mobile computing of using a distributed model

Web-based applications versus client–server applications

There used to be two kinds of distributed software: web-based and client–server-based. Boundaries are beginning to blur though. Some software is part client and part web based. But to compare the differences let's look at a more traditional model.

As you know, client–server software is run internally on your own computer network linked to the server on your own system or on the web. But web-based software (sometimes called hosted) is totally on an applications service provider's (ASP) network on the web. As with any comparisons, there are advantages and disadvantages for each:

- Web-based software is usually paid for on a subscription or usage basis, allowing companies to pay only for what they need and to grow into the system without large up-front costs. Web-based hardware, operating system and database software are also included in the price of the application. Access requires a constant internet connection.
- Client–server software is usually paid for up-front and the initial cost of the system can be high. You are in control of upgrades and don't have to update to the latest version if you don't want to. But you have to manage your systems and pay for technical support. Applications tend to run faster when they are local to the user's computer.

Chapter 26
The use of computer technology in society

Specification coverage

- Effectiveness and impact of computing solutions in society

Learning outcomes

- You should be able to evaluate the effectiveness of computer programs and solutions.
- You should be able to evaluate the impact of, and issues related to, the use of computer technology in society.

Introduction

Some countries have changed so much as a result of technology that answering a simple question about the uses of computing in society is a difficult task. The first computers were designed to perform very specific tasks. Modern computing invades the whole of our lives; even society itself is redefined by the use of social media driven by microprocessors. The terms 'friend' and 'follower' have even been redefined by social network sites such as Facebook and Twitter.

Before the microprocessor, phones were fixed by cables to the wall, now they are portable, multi-functional computing devices that interact with the world in ways never conceived of just a few years ago.

But it is not everywhere in the world that this has happened. Even in countries such as the UK where the technological revolution exists, some people do not have access to this technology. This could be either because they do not have the skills to use it or because they don't have the money to buy it. This has led to what is called the 'social divide' both within developed countries like the UK and, of course, across the globe when comparing developed countries with developing countries.

But it is not only the social divide that is a concern to some people. The fact that modern computing devices such as smartphones even track the location of the user worries some civil rights activists.

Computing development has some very positive impacts on our lives and on society, and also some negative impacts. In this chapter we will explore some of these issues.

Task

Explore the term 'digital divide'.

Question

Discuss the way that the digital divide is affecting people's lives around the world.

Effectiveness of computing solutions

In an earlier chapter we looked at the effectiveness of a solution in terms of matching the design specification. The whole process was neatly contained within a project with a defined start and finish. But to fully evaluate the effectiveness of a program or solution we need to look at its real use and benefits in society.

Medical advances using computing

Some of the biggest advances in the use of computers in society have been in medicine. It is not only advances in monitoring equipment that have revolutionised medical treatments but the use of microprocessors in everything from artificial limbs to communication devices using eye movements and blow straws. The most controversial use of computing relates to implants. This is where a microprocessor is put inside the human body. Early implants were used in things like pacemakers that control the heartbeat. Today, implants can be connected to the human brain or nervous system.

If we look at the development of one such device, people who suffered hearing loss originally used hearing aids. These hearing aids have become smaller and more effective due to computing. Modern hearing aids even link via Bluetooth technology to mobile phones and televisions. However, these devices sit outside the body. A cochlear implant is an implanted electronic hearing device; it connects to the nerves and works by electrically stimulating the nerves inside the person's inner ear. Cochlear implants usually include two main components. The first is an externally worn microphone, sound processor and transmitter system. The second is an implanted receiver and electrode system; something that contains electronic circuits that receive signals from the external system and send electrical currents to the person's inner ear. New systems even connect directly to the nerves sending signals to the brain.

In 1998, Kevin Warwick, a Professor of Cybernetics at Reading University, became the world's first cyborg. He had a radiofrequency device implanted in his arm so that doors in his lab automatically opened and he was able to switch lights on and off using signals from his nervous system. He is also growing a biological brain using brain cells on a microchip.

A device called the Utah array has successfully been connected directly to the human brain. It is called a neural implant.

The advantages of human–computer interfaces are obvious. The brain can be enhanced by connecting to computing devices, and many illnesses and disabilities could be overcome. You could have super-mathematical abilities or a superb memory with the help of a brain transplant. But do we lose our individuality as a result? Is it fair that some people will have enhanced abilities because they can afford it and others cannot? Who controls what you are: you or the processor?

Task

Explore some of the latest medical advances that have been driven by technology.

Question

Discuss the benefits and drawbacks of medical advances using computing.

Changes in shopping due to computing

In the past few years there have been some major changes in the way we shop due to new online shopping environments being launched, coupled with the expanding availability of superfast broadband to people's homes. This now means that people can sit at home and buy the things that they want incredibly conveniently.

The ease with which people can now shop has caused a big shift in the products that shoppers most desire. Recent statistics have shown that technology such as tablet computers and home communication packages (television/broadband/phone) are the most wanted items by people living in the UK.

As shopping websites, social media sites and marketing emails can be accessed from tablet computers and phones, it has altered the way companies try to sell to their potential customers. These days, businesses are attempting to use e-commerce, m-commerce (mobile shopping) and f-commerce (shopping through Facebook) to tempt consumers to buy their products.

Unlike shops in your local town or city, online stores are open 24 hours a day, seven days a week, and this appears to have had an impact on the time of day when people shop. A recent study by an online store has shown that the greatest number of people browsing and purchasing items is between the times of 8p.m. and 10p.m.

Studies have also shown that there has been a big increase in consumers making purchases when they are away from home using smartphones and tablet computers. In the first three months of 2012, 8.2% of all British online transactions were conducted on a mobile device. This was an amazing 2000% rise compared with the first three months in 2010.

Social networking has had a huge impact on the way we shop, such as the way people exchange currency in order to buy the items they want. Facebook now uses 'Facebook credits' to buy virtual products within its games and 'apps'. Interestingly, purchases within applications are becoming a popular way of avoiding advertisements, gaining access to additional content and extra features. In the USA, the picture-sharing social media site Pinterest has become responsible for encouraging more people to visit shopping sites than Facebook.

Social media have also provided companies with alternative methods of engaging with their customers. Companies are learning that if they genuinely respond to customer comments on social media sites or promote special offers through them, they encourage trust and establish a relationship with their customers who potentially respond by promoting their brand to others on the social network.

Technology has had a huge impact on the buying habits of the British people, and as a consequence of this businesses are changing their marketing methods accordingly to take advantage of this change.

Task

List all of the technology-driven products that are used at a supermarket checkout.

Question

Discuss the benefits and drawbacks of online shopping when compared to high street shopping.

Changes in social networking due to computing

Every day, social media are changing the way we communicate and interact and are even playing an important motivational role in getting people involved in political and social debates.

People use social networking sites in order to participate and engage more in educational courses outside work so that they can increase their knowledge, skills and understanding as a way to potentially get a better job.

An increasing number of people are becoming involved in online political, environmental or humanitarian organisations by engaging in debates and signing online petitions. Through social networks more people are becoming involved in community and local issues. This is particularly interesting in certain areas of the world as it could assist groups that are potentially at risk of social exclusion such as immigrants.

Companies are also using social media to engage with potential consumers when they are developing new products or services, enquiring about what they like and what they don't like about products. Asking for suggestions on prototypes and engaging with focus groups to assist in finding the right way to progress when developing new product ranges makes the process more efficient and targeted, as well as dramatically reducing development costs. As mentioned above, companies are also using social networking to publicise and market themselves and their products or services.

Governments and politicians are using social media to encourage more citizen involvement in social and public life in an attempt to appear more transparent and to gain more trust from the electorate.

The increasing use of social media also raises certain issues such as a new digital divide between people who have the skills and understanding to fully exploit the benefits of social networking and those who do not. There are also the ever-potential risks to personal safety, security and privacy, due to the large amounts of personal information that people are placing on social networking sites, some without the taking advantage of the security facilities that all of the sites offer.

Real versus virtual worlds

Recent research studies have increasingly suggested that the gap between our real world and the virtual world is significantly decreasing. Some social scientists now say that we have reached a point where we are no longer looking on our online and offline experiences as separate.

If this is true then it raises new considerations and it may require us to adopt fresh thinking to understand the impact and influence technology is having on our daily lives.

In South Korea, Tesco, the supermarket chain, has installed branches of 'virtual stalls' in commuter railway stations with images of physical shelves that appear on 2D screens. Consumers then shop via the screens, using their smartphones to scan the QR codes (advanced bar codes) and purchase their groceries. Tesco then delivers the provisions to its customers' homes. This type of shopping brings together the ease and convenience of online shopping with the real feel of shopping within a physical supermarket.

In the virtual world of 'Second Life', participants now purchase virtual houses with real money. When some people play games on social networking sites they have such an impact that they will do things like get up in the middle of the night to tend to virtual crops to stop them from decaying.

Another aspect where the boundaries of the real and virtual worlds have been muddied is with geotagging. This is the process of marking a video, photo or other media with a geographical location. So, you have the virtual cyberspace entities of video, images and so on connected with real-world physical locations.

Task

Research the growth in social media over the past 10 years.

Question

Discuss the social changes that have been brought about as a result of social media and the virtual world.

Chapter 27
The controlled assignment

All GCSEs now have a controlled assessment rather than coursework. Controlled assessment is similar to coursework in many ways and it gives you an opportunity to show what you know about a certain topic or area of your subject.

Controlled assessment, however, is different from traditional coursework because it has controls which determine how and where you complete your assessments and what resources you may use. These controls mean that:

- all students complete their assessments in the same way
- assessments are fairer and more reliable
- you get the marks you deserve.

Your teacher will prepare you for the controlled assessment tasks and they will give you any advice and support that you need, such as how and where to research information. By way of guidance, it is recommended that you keep a research diary or folder in which you can:

- make a note of all the resources that you use in your research
- keep your notes, ideas and essay plans together in a portfolio
- record your group work, as you may be allowed to work in groups on certain activities
- record your teacher's feedback and advice to you at certain stages during your assessment.

Your teacher will explain what reference materials and resources you may use and how your assessments have to be completed.

It is really important that you follow these rules:

- Only hand in work that is your own.
- Don't allow other students to copy your work.
- Always credit the author when you have copied work directly from books, the internet or other sources.
- Don't hand in work typed or word-processed by someone else without saying so.

Controlled assessment in Computer Science

In this course you will be assessed through 50 hours of controlled assessment. This will be divided equally into two tasks, so you will have 25 hours for each. The controlled assessment is worth 60 per cent of the total marks. You will have to choose two tasks from a choice of four. Different tasks will be provided by AQA each year.

Working independently, you will need to demonstrate your ability to code a solution to a given problem. The tasks will be set in contexts such as gaming, web and mobile phone applications. You may complete and submit your tasks on paper or electronically.

If you have any questions or concerns about controlled assessment you should always talk to your teacher.

Chapter 28
The examination paper

The examination is worth 40 per cent of the total marks. The examination is 1 hour and 30 minutes long and will be completed in one timetabled session.

The examination will be available as either an on-screen test or a hard-copy question paper. You will need to ask your teacher which form your examination is going to take.

All of the questions within the examination will be compulsory and will be taken from across the subject content.

The examination will include a range of question types requiring short and extended answers.

Glossary

API   Application Programming Interface. The key word is 'interface'. An interface is a common boundary between two separate systems. It is the way that codes on two different systems can communicate with each other.

Array   A type of variable, but it's more like creating a box containing a group of variables within it. Unlike simple variables, arrays can contain more than one piece of data.

Assigning   To set or reset a value that can then be stored in the storage location(s) denoted by the variable name. In most computer programming languages, assignment statements are one of the most important statements.

Asynchronous   Where an action, data or communication occurs randomly and therefore not at regular intervals.

Bootstrap loader   A program that exists in the computer's memory. It is automatically executed by the processor when the computer is switched on.

Buffer   A temporary storage area, usually but not always, in RAM. The main purpose of a buffer is to act as a holding area, enabling the computer to manipulate data before transferring it to a device.

Client–server model   Even on the internet you are in a client–server model. The place where the code is stored is called a web server and you are the client.

Cloud computing   Using linked computing resources (hardware and software) over a network, usually the internet. Cloud computing is based on remote systems containing your data, software and social media systems.

Compiled   A computer program, which has been compiled meaning translated into machine code using a compiler.

Compiler   A special program that processes the lines of code you have written in your chosen programming language by turning them into the machine language or 'code' that the system's processor uses.

Concurrently   Happening at the same time as something else.

Constants   Store values, but as the name implies, those values remain constant throughout the execution of an application.

Database relationships   Comparing data in key fields.

Iteration   A technique for repeating an instruction as a means of getting an answer. For example, if you want to know how many 3s there are in 20, then keep subtracting 3 from 20 until there are none left over. Iteration is associated with loops. Most programming languages have various types of loop commands to perform iteration.

Loops   A common feature in computer programming languages. They are used to repeat a given series of commands until a certain condition or conditions are met.

Negations   In programming these are either: (1) to show something to be false; (2) to cause something to be invalid or (3) to cause something to have no effect.

Parallel   A form of computation in which many calculations are carried out simultaneously, operating on the principle that large problems can often be divided into smaller ones, which are then solved concurrently.

Print   It is important to know that when we say print in a piece of code we don't actually mean print. The PHP engine never actually prints anything, it just displays it on your screen.

Procedure   A block of code that performs a task without returning a value.

Procedures and functions   Named blocks of code that can be used and reused to perform specific tasks.

Processor   A CPU is a type of processor that runs the system. The name processor is a more generic term but is often used to mean the same thing. The only problem with using the term processor when referring to the CPU is that there will be other processors in a computing system but only one CPU.

Rectify   To locate and correct errors in a computer program code.

Robust   In computing terms, robustness is the resilience of the system under stress or when confronted with invalid input. For example, an operating system is considered robust if it operates correctly when it is low on memory or storage space but keeps on functioning normally.

Serial   A serial usually refers to action or existence in a series.

Source code   The actual code programmers use to write a program. It relates to all programming languages. When you write your own programs you will write the source code.

Synchronous   Actions, data or communications happening at regular intervals.

Syntax   In computer science, the syntax of a programming language is the set of rules that define the combinations of symbols that are considered to be the correct symbols for the programming language.

Variables   The contents, or values, of variables will change as users interact with the programs they write. This is why they are called variables.

Virtual   Simulated or extended by computer software or existing on or by means of computers. For example, virtual memory on a hard disk, virtual discussions on the internet or a virtual world in a game.

Volatile   In computing, volatile is not retaining data when electrical power is turned off.

WiFi   Wireless fidelity. A method of transmitting data wirelessly using radio waves.

Wireless hotspot   A place where you can connect to WiFi. Many public places now have these hotspots.

Index